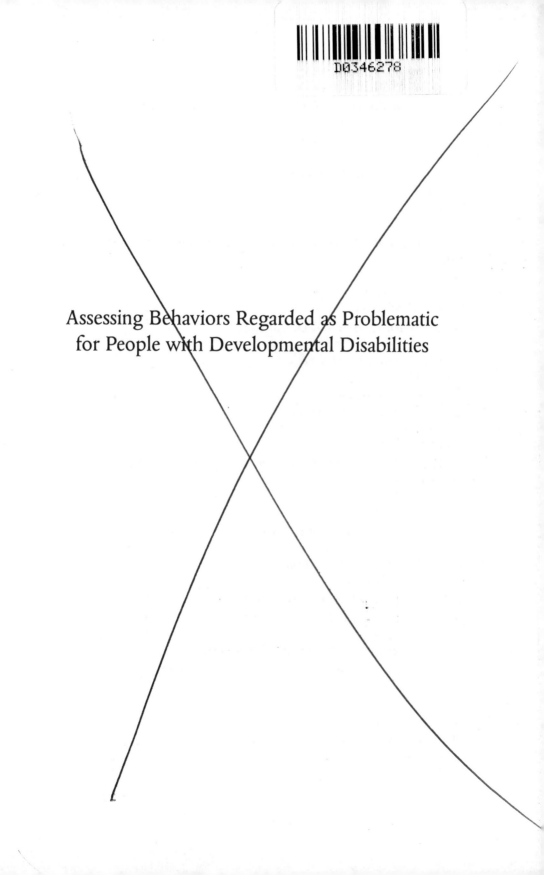

Assessing Behaviors Regarded as Problematic
for People with Developmental Disabilities

of related interest

Behavioural Concerns and Autistic Spectrum Disorders
Explanations and Strategies for Change
John Clements and Eva Zarkowska
ISBN 1 85302 742 1

Raising a Child with Autism
A Guide to Applied Behaviour Analysis for Parents
Shira Richman
ISBN 1 85302 910 6

Transition and Change in the Lives of People with Intellectual Disabilities
Edited by David May
ISBN 1 85302 863 0
Research Highlights in Social Work 38

Women with Intellectual Disabilities
Finding a Place in the World
Edited by Rannveig Traustadottir and Kelley Johnson
ISBN 1 85302 846 0

Asperger's Syndrome
A Guide for Parents and Professionals
Tony Attwood
ISBN 1 85302 577 1

Understanding and Working with the Spectrum of Autism
An Insider's View
Wendy Lawson
ISBN 1 85302 971 8

Pervasive Developmental Disorder
An Altered Perspective
Barbara Quinn and Anthony Malone
ISBN 1 85302 876 2

Lifemaps of People with Learning Disabilities
Barry Gray and Geoff Ridden
ISBN 1 85302 690 5

Asperger Syndrome Employment Workbook
An Employment Workbook for Adults with Asperger Syndrome
Roger N. Meyer
ISBN 1 85302 796 0

A Supported Employment Workbook
Individual Profiling and Job Matching
Steve Leach
ISBN 1 84310 052 5

Assessing Behaviors Regarded as Problematic for People with Developmental Disabilities

by John Clements with Neil Martin

Jessica Kingsley Publishers
London and Philadelphia

The right of John Clements and Neil Martin to be identified as authors of this work has been asserted by them in accordance with the Copyright, Designs and Patents Act 1988.

First published in the United Kingdom in 2002
by Jessica Kingsley Publishers Ltd
116 Pentonville Road
London N1 9JB, England
and
325 Chestnut Street
Philadelphia, PA 19106, USA

www.jkp.com

Copyright © 2002 John Clements and Neil Martin

Library of Congress Cataloging-in-Publication Data
Clements, John, 1946-
   Assessing behaviors regarded as problematic for people with developmental disabilities
/ John Clements with Neil Martin.
      p. Cm.
   Includes bibliographical references and index.
   ISBN 1-85302-998-X (pbk. : Alk. Paper)
      1. Developmentally disabled--Psychology--Case studies. 2. Developmentally
disabled--Social conditions--Case studies. 3. Interpersonal relations--Case studies. 4.
Behavioral assessment--Case studies. I. Martin, Neil, 1963- II. Title.
HV1570 .C54 2002
362.1'968--dc21

2002070920

British Library Cataloguing in Publication Data
A CIP catalogue record for this book is available from the British Library

ISBN 1 85302 998 X

Printed and Bound in Great Britain by
Athenaeum Press, Gateshead, Tyne and Wear

Contents

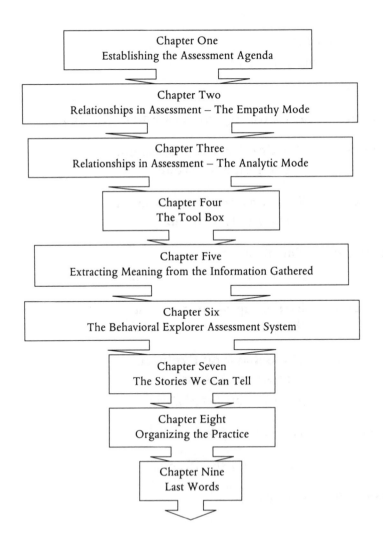

For LesleyAnne

Acknowledgements

This book would never have been produced without the unwavering support of my wife LesleyAnne. She has constantly challenged and stimulated my thinking, 'cheered on' the production and borne without malice the absences and the moodiness that come with this particular territory. It is an enormous debt that I owe her, a fact to which she has only occasionally alluded!

I would also like to thank my collaborator on this project, Neil Martin. Without his tremendous expertise in software development this book could not have incorporated consideration of computer assistance in the assessment process. He has generously provided his psychological expertise by reading and commenting on earlier drafts of the text and he is also responsible for the graphical aspects of the text. Truly a 'universal man'!

My professional debts as a psychologist are wide ranging and I cannot hope to mention all those who have played a part in shaping my understanding and competence. My personal hero remains the late Professor Jack Tizard who pioneered so much psychological work in the field of developmental disabilities and who demonstrated the perfect compatibility of respect for people and respect for science. More immediate influences come from contemporary professional colleagues, some of whom I know personally, some more indirectly, through their writings – Ted Carr, Bryan Craig, Gary LaVigna, Chris Oliver, Al Pfadt and Ewa Zarkowska are all people from whom I have learned much. Since moving to California I have been fortunate enough to be exposed to people who have, very gently, forced me to confront some of the deeper issues involved when we enter the lives of people with developmental disabilities. They have helped me to get behind the slogan 'person centered' and grapple with what it really means. I am grateful to Bill Allen, Claudia Bolton, Michael Smull, Steve Sweet and Dema Garelick for that particular 'assist'.

Which takes me to 'the people' – those people who we say have developmental disabilities, their families and the staff paid to provide supports. What I have learned from books and professional colleagues only makes sense in the context of the profound influence exerted by 'the people' with whom I have worked over the last 30 years. I can only hope that I have given something in return for what I have received. In the specific context of this book I am grateful to the three families who involved me in the lives of their children and who have allowed me to reproduce some of the written documentation that emerged from our work together.

This last point raises a difficult ethical issue. The reports and plans reproduced here were paid for by public monies – likewise, some of the early development work on the Behavioral Explorer package. It would be inappropriate that I profit further from this work. It is difficult to find an exact measure of 'fair', so I have opted for a crude metric. Fifty percent of the royalties from this book will be donated to two organizations that advocate strongly for families and for quality lives for people with developmental disabilities – The California Alliance for Inclusive Communities and Parents Helping Parents (Santa Clara, California).

I would like to pay a special tribute to my lifelong friend Peter Messent. Although our professional interests would appear quite different, his gentle guidance in the field of literature has greatly enriched my broader understanding of the issues that arise in my professional work. His academic productivity has been an inspiration, his comradeship has been an enormous support, his fridge has always had beer in it!

Finally I would like to thank Jessica Kingsley and the team at JKP. It is not just the practical and problem solving support that I appreciate but their quiet confidence in my ability to 'get this thing done'.

John Clements

Preface

This book is about assessment, often considered a rather dry subject. It is also about passions – a passion to understand, to solve mysteries, to detect what may not be obvious, to piece together answers from scattered clues. A passion to find practical ways of helping people move on from dealing with their issues in destructive ways. It is hoped that some of the passion is communicated alongside the more mundane practicalities.

The book has been written primarily for people who are paid to enter the lives of the people that we identify as having developmental disabilities. It is hoped that anyone in this position who is trying to make sense of behavioral challenges and who has experience and some training will find the book useful. It is written for these staff, working in 'ordinary' settings – the schools, residential services, education, employment and leisure services where most people identified as developmentally disabled spend much of their lives. It is not targeted to more specialist research and academic settings or to staff with extensive amounts of higher education. It is not targeted to professional psychologists, although those in training might find some of it useful.

It is therefore hoped that this book will help ordinary staff working in ordinary settings make better sense of the behavioral challenges that they face. It is hoped that a better understanding will in turn lead to more effective supports. If these two hopes are realized, then it is hoped that there will be less demand for the more specialized settings where people with behavioral challenges are congregated – for these are settings where hope often turns to despair.

CHAPTER I

Establishing the Assessment Agenda

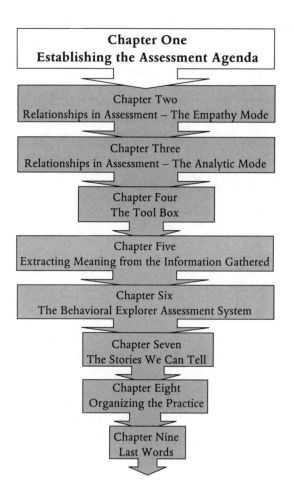

People with developmental disabilities can on occasions behave in ways that others, and sometimes themselves, regard as problematic. This book is about what we do to make sense of those behaviors so that we can support an individual more effectively. It becomes useful once the problem in question becomes formally identified – formally in the sense that there is a widespread acknowledgement that the behavior is problematic; formally also in the sense that resources will be allocated to assessing the problem, to establishing a written plan that is intended to resolve the problem and to implementing that plan. However, such formal identification raises many issues that are important to consider before we look in detail at the tools of assessment.

Human behavior – some general considerations

We all trouble each other to a greater or lesser degree.

Exercise 1.1 Your troublesome behavior

- List the behaviors that you do/have done that other people would regard as problematic.

- Identify the most recent occasion that you behaved in one of these ways.

- Was the most recent incident in the last:

    ○ 24 hours

    ○ week

    ○ month

    ○ six months

    ○ year or longer?

- How does this frequency compare with the frequency of the behaviors of the people with developmental disabilities that you know?

This is a lighthearted exercise and most of the behaviors to which people admit might be regarded as 'minor irritants' (although I am not sure that the colleagues, partners or children of the reader would necessarily agree with that rating!). At a serious level, we know that the true rate of violence, abuse and deception in intimate relationships is frighteningly high and often unknown outside of the circle of intimacy – it is not publicly acknowledged or measured. Thus social relating in the real world involves a range of behaviors and emotions. Just because one person's behavior is troublesome to another does not justify professional engagement to effect change. It will depend in part upon how serious the impact is and the standards that apply amongst the social group/culture in question. However, it is important also to recognize that even when a problem is acknowledged as serious and unacceptable by general standards, it will usually be the case that at least the individual, and perhaps others who are involved, has to agree with that evaluation and agree to participate in the process of change. Unless personal rights are legally removed, consent is a key issue. It remains the case that many people refuse to engage with systematic, profession-alized efforts at change for behaviors that others have identified as problematic. Many people refuse to go along with advice to change their diets or do more exercise. They do not complete courses of prescribed treatment. They refuse to give up their favorite addictions – cigarettes, alcohol, caffeine, chocolate…to name but a few. They refuse to go to class or therapy to learn how to be better communicators, get in touch with their feelings or manage their anger better. They may even deny that what they do is a problem – they may have the audacity to suggest that the real problem lies elsewhere or that if someone has a problem with their behavior, that is his problem. Just because someone else says that our behavior is problematic does not automatically lead to professional engagement for change…in the real world.

In that world, for behavioral issues to be formally addressed requires that the behavior be of sufficient social significance and that the individual agree to participate in that process. Failing that agreement, the only option is to go to law to effect 'compulsory treatment' and that will only be successful in extreme circumstances.

Some special problems for people with developmental disabilities

Powerlessness

A lot of people like to talk. There is a strong preference for communicating through verbal language in one form or another (speaking, writing, reading). Problems are often raised, wrestled with and resolved in the context of verbal dialog. To be without words is to be without influence in many current societies. Developmental disabilities impact most severely in the realm of verbal communication. They impact the capacity to process verbal input, the capacity to produce verbal output, the capacity to formulate verbally thoughts, feelings and interpretations. Thus when a verbally fluent person says that a less articulate person has a problem, it is hard for the individual so identified to challenge that opinion, to explain the situation, to put a point of view in a way that is likely to influence what is being said about him. It is therefore very easy for the judgments of others to determine what happens in that individual's life. The power of the judgment of others is far greater in the life of a person with developmental disabilities than it is in the lives of other people.

This 'intrinsic' disadvantage is compounded by some of the social stories that others weave into the labels that are applied to people with developmental disabilities. They are regarded as stupid, irrational, child-like, incapable of thinking and solving problems. Thus even if the individual can voice an opinion it is likely to be discounted – it will be seen as lacking in sense compared with the opinions of others. It may influence little of what happens.

People with disabilities are also likely to be poor. They are very likely to be unemployed or, at best, hold down a minimum wage job. Even though considerable sums of public money may be spent on providing services to such individuals, they are unlikely to have control over those monies. In many societies power and money are closely linked. As a poor person the individual with developmental disabilities will find it hard to choose who provides services to her – who supports her on a day-to-day basis, who provides health care, with which psychologist or psychiatrist does she feel comfortable working. It will be hard to seek a second opinion. People with developmental disabilities are generally expected to accept what they are given by others – and often they are also expected to be grateful for it.

Thus people identified as developmentally disabled are robbed of many of the resources that the rest of us rely on for decision making and control in our everyday lives. They have less knowledge and information, they have less money, they have fewer choices and those that they make are often less respected. They are relatively powerless and are socially devalued. In such a context it is all too easy for powerful others to determine what happens in people's lives, to an extent that none of the rest of us would accept for ourselves.

> *If the behavior guy says I have to earn a soda rather than just having it in the fridge, that is what happens. If the legalized drug dealer says that I should take this pill then that is what will happen, and if I spit it out it will be buried in my ice cream (that is if I am allowed ice cream and have not been put on a calorie controlled diet by a bunch of overweight suits calling themselves 'the team').*

It does not stop there.

A life of constant scrutiny

Many people who use services for people with developmental disabilities have need of a lot of support as they go about their everyday lives. This has its blessings but the downside is that your life is under the microscope. You are scrutinized 24 hours a day, 7 days a week, 365 days a year. Almost everything you do is observed and a lot of it will get written down and passed around so that 'everybody knows'. Just imagine this in your own life – what list of inappropriate behaviors would emerge, especially once your home, workplace, local bar and vacation spot were all communicating with each other (for consistency of course!). The more time you spend closely observing any human being, the more problematic behavior you are likely to observe and the less likely you are to see those calm, communicating, rational problem solvers that we all delude ourselves into believing that we really are.

A life of sometimes dismal quality

People with disabilities lack key resources, including money, and are stigmatized, devalued and scrutinized to death. The lives that they lead are often not ones that they would ever choose for themselves; they are the ones that others choose for them. Quality of life – both objective and subjective – is an important influence over human functioning. Disadvantage, deprivation and lack of control raise the likelihood that any human will resort to behavior that goes against the norms of (such an oppressive) society. 'Disabilityland' is a low rent sector and when you work with people so identified you work with a relatively disadvantaged group. This is a topic to which we will return when considering assessment in more detail. It is important at this stage to flag up the necessity of not seeing the individual in isolation from both the immediate social context and from the broader ways in which society is organized.

Thus people with developmental disabilities are much more likely than others to be identified as having problematic behavior, for that identification to become public and for it to be followed by professionalized efforts at change, efforts that will intrude themselves into people's lives, whether they like it or not. Coercion is an iceberg, the tip of which is an incident report on the desk of a 'protective services' investigator.

This is not to deny that there are individuals who do have serious behavioral and emotional difficulties and that these difficulties are often quite long term. They impact tremendously upon the individual's own quality of life and they often also intrude upon the rights of others in very significant ways. They deserve serious consideration and it is hoped that this book will contribute to defining what 'serious consideration' might mean. However, great care is needed about publicly identifying someone in this way – such a public identification establishes for the individual a 'reputation' and adds to the burden of stigma. Careful consideration must be given to justifying planned, professionalized involvement in the behavioral issues for people with developmental disabilities.

The justification process

The basis for identification

The behavior that is the focus of concern must meet some standard of 'significantly unacceptable'. A behavior would be significantly unacceptable if it meets at least one of the following criteria:

- It is illegal and the law concerned is usually enforced.

- If anyone else did this there would be sustained efforts by those involved with the person to effect change.

- The behavior is likely to inflict demonstrable costs on the life of the person.

- The behavior is likely to inflict demonstrable costs on the lives of others who have a right to be free from such imposed costs.

In addition, if the involvement of specialist professionals is sought:

- The behavior should be continuing despite informal efforts to draw the problem to the person's attention and to effect some change.

It is also important at this stage for all those involved to understand that identifying a concern is not the same as identifying the area for change. Just because the individual is identified as functioning in a socially problematic way does not imply that it is only the individual that has to change. In professionalizing the issue all parties are implicitly agreeing to follow through on what the assessment identifies as influences and areas for change. This may mean change in those who have identified the problem and how they do things. Unless everyone is clear about this and in agreement with it at the outset, then professionalizing the issue will lead to targeting only the individual for change. Down that road lies oppression.

A mechanism for consent

As for anyone else, unless one is prepared to go for legal commitment and compulsory change (necessary occasionally) then the individual must have a powerful voice at the decision making table. If the individual has difficulty speaking for herself or is judged incompetent to decide on the issues, then some form of substituted consent process must be available. The voice of the consent needs to be powerful and independent of as many vested interests as possible. Sometimes this voice may be legally established – parents for underage children, legal guardians or conservators. Sometimes the voice may be informally recognized – a best friend, a trusted relative, an independent advocate. The American Association on Mental Retardation (AAMR) Guidebook on Consent provides a good overview on this topic from a United States perspective (Dinerstein, Herr and O'Sullivan 1999). However, there are psychological as well as legal issues. A good quality decision is likely to emerge when there is a balance of power and a lack of control by those with vested interests. From this point of view, irrespective of what the law permits, substituted consent should never come from those directly impacted by the behavior or from those who make their living from 'treating' behavior (psychologists, psychiatrists, behavior analysts, therapists). It is recognized that in many service contexts such independent consent mechanisms are not available. This serves as a reminder of the importance attached to developing such mechanisms.

Thus if the behavior can be regarded as significantly unacceptable, if consent has been obtained and if all understand that they are signing up to an enterprise whose outcomes are uncertain (as to who or what has to change), then we are justified in taking steps to assess the behavior and to develop relevant interventions for change.

Before we proceed with these matters, there are a number of other issues to comment upon – issues that will influence both what we do and how we do it.

Clarifying the outcomes

Behavior

Our justification will have identified certain behaviors as 'significantly unacceptable'. They may be unacceptable in and of themselves (for example, arson, child molestation), so that they are behaviors for which there is zero tolerance. They may be unacceptable in terms of their frequency – occasional outbursts of shouting and screaming would be tolerable but not several outbursts a day. They may be unacceptable in terms of duration – a one-second scream might pass little noticed but not a three-hour bout. The behaviors may be unacceptable in terms of their severity or intensity. If you just scratched a little when you got anxious no one would bother, but if you rip your face, arms and legs to pieces then a change is needed. Thus one outcome of the work that we undertake should be that the behaviors in question change in some kind of measurable way – change in frequency, duration and/or severity. However, in light of earlier comments about the disadvantaged status of people with developmental disabilities and the fact that the justification criteria raise quality of life issues, behavior change alone is a necessary but not sufficient specification of the desired outcomes.

Quality of life

When considering what we hope to achieve we also need to identify how behavior change impacts quality of life. If part of the justification for intervening is that the behavior is causing the individual's life to be restricted (not going to preferred places or activities, not having supportive relationships) then there should be evidence that if the behavior change occurs, restrictions or losses decrease. It is not going to be acceptable if the individual's behavior changes but he continues to lead an unnecessarily restricted life. In addition, quality of life should be seen as having an independent value as an outcome. It should be part of what we are striving for. Given the disadvantaged status of people with developmental disabilities, every opportunity should be taken to leverage improvements in quality of life. Given that behavioral work will usually involve an investment of resources, this should be seen as an opportunity to improve matters in general. Thus from many points of view, quality of life has to be seen as a key outcome, in addition to the specific behavioral outcomes discussed above.

Behavior stability

The issues with which this book is concerned are, by definition, socially significant. The behaviors in question exact tremendous costs upon the individual and others. They generate enormous emotional concerns. It would be nice if they could be dealt with once and for all. Unfortunately, human behavior is not stable. It reflects the operation of a myriad of variables within the individual and in the external environment (see Chapter 3). Effecting change is like juggling and, when all is well, the balls stay in the air. But a shift in wind speed or atmospheric pressure, a lapse in concentration, a distraction from the audience, a loss of light, some inherent dynamic property of the ball...and the balls fall to earth. Our efforts at change should be directed at effecting change in a way that will last as long as possible. However, changing behavior is not like treating a curable disease or delivering a 100 percent effective vaccination. It is a much more unstable enterprise. Our hope is for long lasting change, and some of the things that we do will raise the likelihood of that, but we should not be surprised or disappointed if at some point in time the behaviors in question recur. If medical analogies bring comfort, then working with behavior is more like dealing with a virus such as herpes. We can deal with it and reduce the likelihood of recurrence, but it is always lurking there and may reappear under a number of circumstances. When it does reappear it can be dealt with again. So it is with behavior. It is important that these understandings form part of our expectations about behavioral work. Change for ever is the exception rather than the rule, even if it is a glorious exception and one to which we will continue to aspire!

Clarifying the process

The sequence

Working towards behavior change can be characterized as a sequence of activities with a number of feedback loops. The sequence is outlined in Figure 1.1.

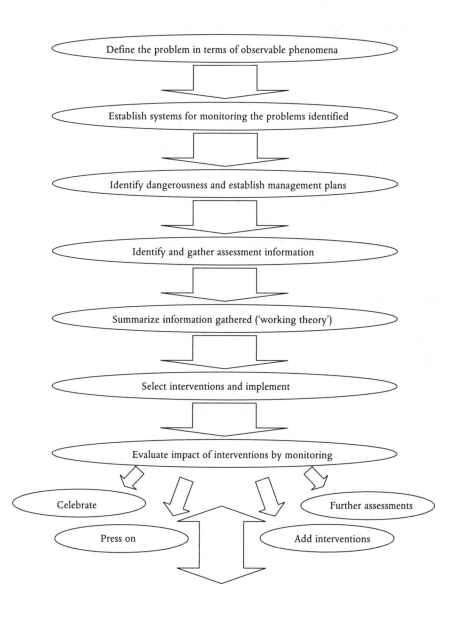

Figure 1.1 Activity sequence for behavior work

The sequence is an algorithm, a structure for guiding the process. It does not mean that there is a meeting for each step in the sequence or special paperwork for each step. The sequence is a way of defining what needs to be done, the bases to cover. How we organize ourselves to deliver that sequence will depend upon the particular situation of the individual and those who support him.

DEFINE THE PROBLEM IN TERMS OF OBSERVABLE PHENOMENA

It is vital to define the focus of concern in terms of things that everyone can see and/or agree upon. Overt behaviors will be part of this (hitting, screaming, breaking things, stealing, sexually assaulting). But important, less readily scrutinized, phenomena may also be part of the picture. Emotions are usually an important part of the concerns – anger, anxiety, sadness, overexcitement. At this stage it is important to unpack what people are meaning when these terms are used and to define them operationally so that we know and agree when people are experiencing these things and whether there has been change in this area. We can do the same sort of work with attitudes, which may be important when the behavior is part of a broader issue such as racism, sexism or child abuse. The broader issues to do with quality of life that we discussed earlier are likely to become clearer through the course of assessment and therefore may not be part of the initial definition of the problem.

ESTABLISH SYSTEMS FOR MONITORING THE PROBLEMS IDENTIFIED

Once the problems are identified, systems must be established for measuring and monitoring the phenomena. This will certainly involve some form of counting behaviors but may also include ratings or some other way of measuring emotional state (for example, psycho-physiological measures). These monitoring systems will form the bedrock of decision making. Our efforts will be judged effective insofar as they lead to significant change in the observable phenomena that we are defining as problematic. We need to have as objective a measure as possible of these phenomena. People's intuitive judgments are not to be trusted. They reflect too many of the issues of the people making the judgments. Also, change is a long-term business and the human capacity for processing data long term is very limited – relying upon our memory of how someone was a year ago compared with now is not likely to be an accurate guide. Finally, and very practically, in many of the human services that support people with developmental disabilities, staff turnover is high. There is simply no way that the current set of people involved can make judgments about change unless there is a clear system for monitoring in place. Effective monitoring systems are a critical component of serving people competently.

IDENTIFY DANGEROUSNESS AND ESTABLISH MANAGEMENT PLANS FOR DANGEROUS INCIDENTS

If the behavioral concerns are such that the individual or others are in serious danger (for example, some types of aggression or self-injury) and no coherent plans have been made for managing such risks, then this is an important area to address early in the sequence. If those who support the individual are extremely anxious about managing incidents and lack confidence in their approach then a number of things follow. There are likely to be more incidents. Those involved will become increasingly desperate for a quick fix that will relieve their concerns. They will find it difficult to invest the time and effort required to assess the problem and to work with plans that will lead to change in the longer term, which is often the nature of psychological approaches. By having thought out, mutually agreed and well rehearsed prevention plans and reactive 'drills' for addressing the dangerousness issue, we build confidence, reduce anxiety and reduce incidents. This helps people to take the longer view and to invest in the kind of work that this book describes.

IDENTIFY AND GATHER ASSESSMENT INFORMATION

This is the focus of the present volume and will be described in subsequent chapters.

SUMMARIZE INFORMATION GATHERED TO A 'WORKING THEORY' THAT DESCRIBES IDENTIFIED CONTRIBUTORS AND HOW THEY INFLUENCE THE PROBLEMS IN QUESTION

This stage is considered in detail in Chapter 5. However, it is important to recognize this as a distinct element in the sequence. A large amount of information may be gathered in the course of carrying out an assessment. This needs to be summarized into an accessible format –

which we have called here a 'working theory' – that draws out the main things learned about likely contributors to the problems identified. If this is not done, then the information gathered may play no role in the decisions made. If nobody knows what to make of the information then decisions about what to do are likely to be based on the intuitive judgments of those currently involved. Such judgments may be based upon personal theories or personal experience and are likely to reflect the views of the most powerful people (not necessarily the smartest) in the group. They will often tell us more about those people than the individual whose behavior is supposed to be of concern. This amounts to a refusal to 'listen' to the individual and negates all that this book regards as important. It is at this stage also that the broader quality of life issues will become clearer and inform the outcomes that we will set ourselves to achieve.

SPELL OUT THE INTERVENTIONS THAT WOULD ADDRESS THE NEEDS IDENTIFIED AND SELECT THOSE INTERVENTIONS THAT WILL BE IMPLEMENTED (BASED UPON IMPORTANCE AND FEASIBILITY)

Once the likely contributors are identified the next step is to spell out all that would need to be done to address these issues. From this ideal intervention plan, those involved will need to select those things that they will commit to actually doing. This decision will be based upon judgments about which contributors are regarded as most important and which plans are feasible to implement in the real world of the individual and those who support her. This will usually leave some interventions for which additional resources may be sought or that remain in a pool of ideas to draw upon if the plans agreed do not lead to effective change.

IMPLEMENT AND EVALUATE IMPACT OF INTERVENTIONS THROUGH THE MONITORING SYSTEM

Plans agreed need to be implemented and their impact evaluated through the monitoring system. Further decisions must be based upon the information generated by this system. The numbers are critical but there will remain matters of judgment – for example, how long to stick with a plan that is not apparently having an impact, whether to add a plan or do more assessment if demonstrable progress is not being made.

The numbers will also need to be supplemented with consideration of the broader quality of life outcomes that emerged as significant during the course of assessment.

It is important at this stage not to miss out on the possibility of celebration! Sometimes the people identified as problematic have so many issues that after one is resolved there are still plenty more to work on. We may forget to celebrate success. Likewise in congregate services there are many individuals whose behaviors give rise to concern and once one person has made progress another person occupies the top priority slot. We may forget to celebrate. Don't!

Managing the process

The above sequence, and this book in general, assumes that there is a process and that it gets 'managed'. The social situation of many people with developmental disabilities can be quite complex – as well as friends and family they are likely to have a lot of people paid to be in their lives. These people will have different job titles and work for different employing organizations. The situations where the individual's life was 'managed' in all its aspects by a single agency are, thankfully, fading into history in many places. However, this often leaves it unclear as to how a process such as that described in this book is to be managed. The point here is that there needs to be someone who is identified and accepted as the person who is coordinating and directing the process. This may be the person regarded as having disabilities, it may be a parent or a person who is in a paid capacity. It is not the case that the coordination and direction should always be in the hands of the person who carries a particular job title ('psychologist', 'behavior analyst', 'case manager'). This may sometimes be appropriate but not always. The key points are that this coordination and direction should be *someone's* job and that this role is acknowledged by all those involved. Leadership is needed so that the sequence outlined earlier is delivered. Who takes that role will be determined by local circumstances, but the role must be occupied. If it is not someone's job it will be no one's job and this will significantly reduce the likelihood of outcomes that are positive for the individual being achieved.

Thus far in the chapter we have moved from important broad social issues around power, control and social status to more practical issues of how we conduct appropriate behavioral work. The chapter will close with a return to those broader social issues.

Clarifying the enterprise – power and relationships revisited

What are we doing in people's lives?

This book is aimed at a practitioner audience – it is aimed at those people who, like the author, are paid to enter the lives of people identified as disabled. We may be paid directly by the person herself, or more likely by some kind of agency charged with providing services to the person. Even if paid directly, the money often originates from taxes paid by many members of society so that there is some accountability to more than just the individual involved.

Being paid to support people in their everyday lives is an odd job. Whatever job title we carry, the expectation seems to be that we do more than just observe or serve in some purely mechanical way. We are charged with playing an active role in the person's life. We seem to be given a 'duty of care' so that as a result of our efforts the person's well-being and interests are advanced. This may involve us challenging and changing the environment and society – for example, if the individual is being discriminated against. It may involve us in trying to challenge and change the individual – for example, to help someone communicate more effectively or to feel better. We are therefore charged with being a change agent and this is where profound issues arise, some of which were touched upon earlier.

That terrible human flaw

Power over others can be a terrible human addiction. The reinforcing value of control over others can be very powerful for many people. As well as the sense of control over others, there are the secondary gains of what can be achieved for you as an individual if you can get other people to do the things that you want done. Sometimes the exercise of power has a positive spin – the notion of the benevolent dictator who controls and directs others for the good of all. Sometimes power over others, if unchecked, delivers disastrous outcomes for others – child abuse, domestic violence, chronic oppression and deprivation, cruel dictatorships and genocide all reflect in part such power dynamics. The perpetrators of these acts are not just the sadistic psychopaths of this world. They are ordinary people who find themselves in extraordinary positions of power. This understanding has helped to drive the development of democracy and the notion of human rights – the urgent need to have systems with checks and balances, the recognition that unchecked power over others is not in the best interests of those others. We recognize also that some groups are especially vulnerable to victimization in this way.

Powerlessness...again

Skills and knowledge can be a source of power, lack of them a major disadvantage. Membership of a privileged, high status group can be a source of power ('good family', 'right skin color', 'right religion', 'good old boy'). Membership of a low status, socially despised group makes you vulnerable...even if you have skills and knowledge. Money is a source of power, lack of it a disadvantage.

So we see what people with learning disabilities, especially if those disabilities are pervasive, are facing. They lack skills and knowledge, they lack money; and in many societies this will automatically make you a member of a low status group. No one wants to be like you. Additional dynamics grow around such a status.

People with disabilities, like many 'outsiders', are readily perceived as a threat to the social order. Threats to the powerful need at best to be controlled and potentially also eliminated. Whilst this is not the place to detail the history of how western society has related to those it identifies as disabled, that history is replete with the idea of threat. The precise form of the threat has reflected the ideology prevailing at the time – the children of the devil, the genetic polluters threatening national deterioration, the economic burdens threatening our health, education and welfare systems. But threat it always is.

How this translates

When we enter the lives of people with disabilities, we come mostly with good intentions, and it is important that we realize those. However, if we are to do so, we have to be aware of the dynamics. We come from the 'other side of the tracks'. Relatively speaking, we come from a privileged position. We are coming to people whom it may be hard to take seriously – after all, they lack all that skill and knowledge and do all sorts of bizarre and irrational things. Beneath all the positive verbal spin, the politically correct speak that surrounds what we do, we are operating in a society that sees people with disabilities as a threat in need of control, sometimes benevolent, sometimes malevolent, but always control. There is much tacit encouragement for us to exercise power over the person with disability. We may not be aware of this and we may find it hard to accept what is being spelled out here. However, we ignore it at the peril of the person identified as disabled.

Nowhere is the danger greater than when we enter the life of a person whose behavior is cause for concern. The behaviors that give rise to concern are clearly powerful in a very naked way. They are a bid for control and a threat. Of all the issues that arise in working for people with developmental disabilities, behavioral issues stimulate a power-based response. Now the subtext rises to the surface, the gloves are off. Those who should be humble and thankful for our kindness have stepped out of line. They have failed to show proper respect for their betters. They need to be taught a lesson.

Frequently they are. All people with disabilities are vulnerable to abuse but none more so than those who challenge us by their behavior. They may be beaten or starved, twisted and tied, rejected and isolated...informally. Formally they may be cattle prodded or technozapped, fined and deprived, flatlined or otherwise subdued with neurosmashing chemicals – and all in the name of 'treatment'.

The struggle

So our entry into people's lives is the start of a struggle. We are setting out on a journey together but we have to be clear who we are for each other. Whatever our job title, at the heart of what we do is the creation of a real relationship with a real other. We have to get close to and to know someone who is, for us, a member of an apparently alien group. We have to discover that the people on 'the other side of the tracks' are not really so different from us. We have to find ways of offsetting our social baggage – to seek an equitable and respectful relationship, and to wrestle with the devil of power. Yet we have to be a force for change. Things should stay good or improve for the other as a result of our participation in the journey.

What models can we have? How should we call ourselves? Friend does not sound right. Partner, in the business sense? Mentor? Coach? Guide? Teacher? Some of us may have a formal role with attached authority (for example, teacher in a society where schooling is compulsory). Most of us have no such formal authority. If we are to let go of the informal authority that we have discussed above, we have to gain and to exercise influence through the relationship that we forge, whatever name we use for this relationship.

So what?

This is not a matter of words – about how a thing shall be called. It is the determining influence about what goes into a book like this. Once we begin to understand ourselves as part of a relationship with real people, fellow travelers, in which influence is exerted 'informally', it has a profound effect on what we look for when we are trying to understand the behavior of the other. Now the life the person has led, the relationships in which she is embedded, her perceptions and priorities, her beliefs and feelings become as important as the more scientific analysis of incidents. A coach has to know the players, not just study the plays. Assessment is not a clinical exercise. It is part of a working, problem solving relationship.

Once we understand the relationship arena in which we operate, it places constraints upon what we do to effect change. The ends do not justify the means and the influence that we exert has to be consonant with the role that we play. The coach cannot beat or lock up the players even if it would make them play better.

This chapter reflects a struggle, not a theory. It is a personal struggle to understand what I am doing in people's lives and to reflect upon the mistakes of the past, my own included. It is not 'right' and it does not provide the 'answer'...but it is to be hoped that it illustrates the importance of the struggle. Assume nothing – question everything.

In the next chapter we examine how we might forge the equitable relationship into which we will incorporate the support that we call 'behavioral'.

CHAPTER 2

Relationships in Assessment – The Empathy Mode

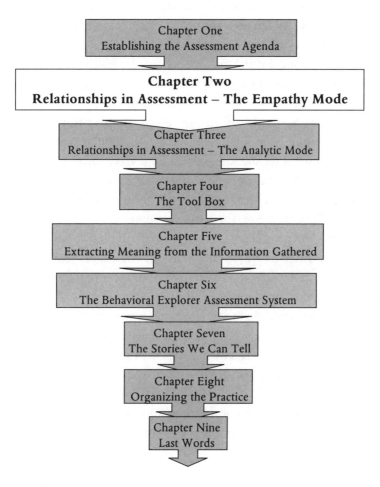

Chapter One
Establishing the Assessment Agenda

Chapter Two
Relationships in Assessment – The Empathy Mode

Chapter Three
Relationships in Assessment – The Analytic Mode

Chapter Four
The Tool Box

Chapter Five
Extracting Meaning from the Information Gathered

Chapter Six
The Behavioral Explorer Assessment System

Chapter Seven
The Stories We Can Tell

Chapter Eight
Organizing the Practice

Chapter Nine
Last Words

In the previous chapter the importance of establishing equitable, respectful relationships was identified generally as an element critical to effective behavioral support. In this chapter the struggle so described is considered more specifically. The readers of this book will play various roles in the lives of those identified as disabled. Some of those roles will involve, by their nature, a disparity in formal power or authority (for example, being a teacher in a country that has universal, compulsory education, being a parent of a younger child, being a nurse in a facility where people are legally detained for compulsory treatment). Others will have no such inbuilt disparity (for example, supporting an adult in that person's own home) although there will be the informal disparities in terms of access to information and social status. Whatever one's role, getting close to making sense of all the factors that contribute to the outcomes that we call 'challenging behavior' means getting close to the reality that the other person experiences. It requires more than just the thinking and technical skills that are considered elsewhere in this book. It requires us to have some sense of who that other person is – what kind of person in general, how events and stimuli are interpreted and experienced, what kinds of things are seen as priorities, what is irrelevant, how the person is feeling at any particular moment in time. Perhaps this is what we mean by empathy (I have never been too sure). Personally, I use the image of a journey that we are making together and the need for us to get to know each other, to create a sense of fellowship, to become fellow travelers, for a time at least.

Whilst the image is clear I have always struggled to know what has to be done in order to create that sense of the other. Tradition would have it that the best way is to talk to someone. Yet verbal behavior is such a slippery medium, so easily shaped by social pressures. At times it can be a most unreliable guide to what the other truly thinks, believes, feels. The preference for verbal communication also assumes that people are aware of and can articulate all that they feel and where those feelings come from – an assumption that is patently false. Thus working with people who do not speak or who find it hard to communicate in words is not a disadvantage when it comes to gaining insight. Rather it forces us to think more clearly about how humans get close to each other's realities.

What follows is not some well-validated approach, guaranteed to deliver an empathy outcome. It is an odd assortment of ideas that may help to forge a sense of the other, given that this is always an uncertain enterprise. The fact that it is uncertain does not diminish its significance in the process of building an understanding.

Clearing the decks

To get close to another means in some way dampening or stilling our own selves and our own issues so that we can be open to the other – an other whose experience, thoughts and feelings may be radically different from our own. We cannot just work by personal analogy – that is, how I would think/feel if I was in that situation, if that happened to me. We have to bridge a gulf opened up by alternative perspectives and the potential experiences of disadvantage, discrimination and oppression. We have to be open to differences and this raises many issues for us.

Go to the mirror

A special education school principal and a teacher stood in front of a coffee machine. It was unfamiliar to them but had a clearly written sequence of instructions. They had got halfway but were not sure how to complete so that a cup of coffee resulted. They stood looking puzzled for a few minutes and then began hitting the machine...

Yet we are the great problem solvers compared with those people who are disabled and cannot think clearly, cannot problem solve and can only act in very concrete ways.

Whenever I consult to organizations about organizational functioning the first complaint is always about communication (as in many other relationships)...

Yet we are the great communicators compared with those people with disabilities who are communicatively impaired.

As I move around the social world outside of disabilityland and as I look around the world today I witness day in day out people acting towards others in grossly insensitive ways...

Yet we allegedly have the great theory of mind capacities that enable us to know how other people think and feel compared with those people with autistic spectrum disorders who are so socially impaired.

We could go on. One of the adaptive illusions that feeds our optimism and keeps us going in this world is the sense that we have of ourselves as competent and managing, rational and problem solving, as being effective and in control. That means denying our stupidities, our incompetences, our insensitivities and the very limited control that we have over events around us. It forces us to distance ourselves from those people who clearly illustrate the parts of ourselves that we are so keen to deny – to regard them as 'disabled' in contrast to our own, 'enabled' selves.

Thus to get close to the other we must get close to our own selves – to go to the mirror and see all that there is to see, both the enabled and disabled reflections. To see it, to accept it…heck, perhaps even to like it. We are who we are, enabled and disabled, and that is OK.

If we cannot get past this, if we cannot see that we are all made up of competences and incompetences, it becomes much harder to get past the notion of 'disabled', to see the other for who she is and to experience fellowship. We may experience pity but that is not the same thing and is of little help in making some sense of the other's reality.

Remove the glasses

A linked element of consciousness-raising concerns the society in which we operate and the views that it holds of those who get publically identified as 'disabled'. This is a topic that we began to consider in Chapter 1. We are all part of a broader social context, with a history and traditions, a set of values – an idea of what is the most valuable human attribute (for example, youth, slimness, intelligence, strength, manners). Societies vary in what is held up as ideal and will tend to devalue and oppress those who do not exemplify those ideals. Those who become outcasts are subject not just to devaluation but to stereotypes about their true nature, which will justify how they are treated. People with disabilities have been variously regarded as children of God or children of the devil, as being subhuman and closer to animals than people, as being a danger to society or a drain on resources, as being perpetual children. Such stereotypes are deeply ingrained and as individuals we are usually not conscious of the views that we have absorbed over the years that we have grown up in our societies.

To get close to the other we need to become aware of the stereotypes that we hold so that we can challenge them. We will not be able to obliterate them 'at a single stroke'. They will gradually dissolve as we get closer and closer to more and more of those individuals who get identified publicly as disabled. However, if we are not aware of these views it is quite likely that we will develop a sense of the other that is more like the social stereotype than the reality of the other.

Clear the personal agendas

When we come to the other we will come with a range of personal agendas. Some of these may be practical – we are under pressure of time and need to come up with answers quickly. Some may be personal – we need to be seen by others as competent, we have to 'succeed'. Some may reflect the role that we perceive ourselves to be playing in other people's lives – we need to keep them in line and show who is in authority, we need to make them happy, we need to make them independent. These things must be recognized for what they are – *our* agendas, *our* needs, *our* preferences. This does not mean that they are irrelevant, incorrect or bad (though they may of course be all of those things!), just that this is our stuff. It gets in the way of knowing the other. If we are not aware of these issues and do not act to set them aside then the story that we tell about the other will likely be one that satisfies our needs rather than one that reflects reality for the other.

What we are struggling for here is an empathy mode in our relationship with the other. We may be in different modes for different activities – our own agendas may rightly dominate in other modes. However, when we are wanting, above all else, to get as close as we can to the other's experiences and reality, then we have to become aware of our agendas and work to set them aside.

All the above contribute to us reaching a point where we are as still and open as we can be to the other. What then?

Taking action

Time together

It may help to spend some time with the other! This is probably best described as 'hanging out'. We need to be with the person in his ordinary everyday life. The more varied the circumstances in which we can be together the better. We may do activities together but it is also helpful to take a more observational role – not in an analytic way (counting, measuring – all that good stuff to which we will turn later), but more in the way of trying to absorb what the person is attending to and how they are reacting to what is going on: what are the things that impact most upon them; what are the issues that they take up with other people; being 'with' the person rather than studying him. This is critical for someone in my position who enters a person's life for the first time at the point of concern about behavior. It is equally important for those who have known the person through living and/or working with him over time but who perhaps have been dominated by another agenda – being a teacher, being a nurse, being a 'support worker'. They also will need some time with the person, freed from that agenda. It matters little whether the person can speak or not. Good listening requires eyes as much as ears.

Reading up

As well as time together it is important to learn as much as possible about the person and her history – to look at the information already available. Some may prefer to do this before spending time with the person, some after. There is no 'right' way. Both activities are necessary. However, in reviewing the information available great care is needed. The lives of people with disabilities often generate a lot of documentation. Much of the material available in charts (files) is a mix of important information, trivia and poorly substantiated opinion. There are often serious omissions. At the early stages of trying to get close to the other, it will be important to focus upon factual information rather than opinion and interpretation. Later we may consider opinion but as we begin the process of trying to get a sense of the other we are going to be more helped by facts – events that happened, reactions observed, verified likes and dislikes, issues that engage the other, that seem important to her, information that is clearly absorbed and information that does not seem to get through, recurring or stable themes over time, changes over time.

Reflecting upon the experience and the information

Having cleared the desks, spent time with the person in 'stillness' and absorbed the information, time is needed to reflect upon this. We need to go over the things that we regard as the facts or information about the person, to process intellectually what this might mean for how the world is experienced and life is lived. We need to reflect emotionally – what feelings does our contact with the person bring out and whose feelings are they? Sometimes the feelings brought out will reveal something about ourselves – some personal passion, preference, prejudice or fear. Sometimes the feelings will reflect the other's feelings – the anger or sadness is theirs. There is no hard and fast way of distinguishing these alternatives – they need to be considered and a tentative judgment made.

This process of reflection may be carried out in a number of ways. Some may prefer to do this in a focused way – giving a block of time to carry this out. Others may prefer to review consciously for a short period what has been learned, leave it be and come back to it two or three times before reaching any interpretation. These are matters of personal style.

The important point is to recognize the need for reflection, to avoid a rush to judgment, to allow the sense of the other to emerge, the empathy to build in a tentative way, rather than seeking the once and for all 'got it' flash of insight.

Concluding remarks

Although empathy is a word that is easy to use and to define, walking the talk seems a lot harder to do with any certainty. From here on in the book we will move in a more surefooted way as we work through the activities that are required to assess behavior and to develop support plans. Yet unless we can gain some real sense of the other and create a bond of fellowship, our ability to make sense of the other and to provide meaningful support will be impaired. It will not be made impossible – the scientific study of behavior has been very fruitful – but on its own it will not reach the level of excellence to which those of us paid to do this work must aspire. I freely admit to being confused and uncertain and I apologize to the reader for spreading that around in this chapter. However, to omit the topic because it is difficult or because I do not have clever answers would be to deny a vital area of practice and to pander to the illusion that scientific, objective analysis is not just necessary but sufficient.

CHAPTER 3

Relationships in Assessment –
The Analytic Mode

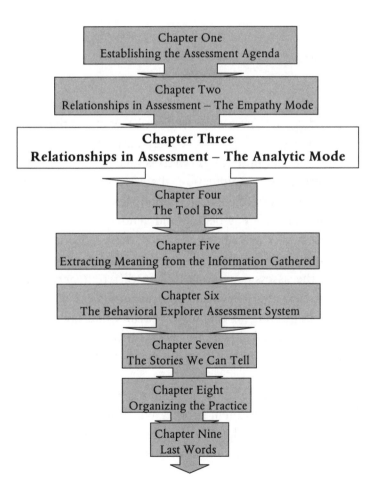

Chapter One
Establishing the Assessment Agenda

Chapter Two
Relationships in Assessment – The Empathy Mode

Chapter Three
Relationships in Assessment – The Analytic Mode

Chapter Four
The Tool Box

Chapter Five
Extracting Meaning from the Information Gathered

Chapter Six
The Behavioral Explorer Assessment System

Chapter Seven
The Stories We Can Tell

Chapter Eight
Organizing the Practice

Chapter Nine
Last Words

In the previous chapter we focused upon the need to get close to the reality of the other person and to create a sense of fellowship. We talked of the 'empathy mode'. In this chapter we consider the 'analytic mode'. Faced with a behavior of concern, we need some systematic way of reviewing potential contributors and identifying those that are relevant to the particular individual. We need a framework that guides us to gather information about the things that most impact human behavioral functioning. These two modes, the empathic and the analytic, inform each other. They go on together. Referring to them as 'modes' is a device for promoting understanding, not necessarily a literal description about how we function. They interact to guide us towards an understanding of the issues for the other person that are indicated by the behavior which gives rise to concern.

Starting points

Be specific

It is important to list out in terms of observable behaviors (things that can be seen and agreed upon, measured even!) what it is that the person does that gives rise to concern. The concern may be expressed by others and/or by the person himself. Fuzzy terms such as outbursts, tantrums, aggression, obsessions, manipulation, disturbance will not do at this stage. Those terms are often used initially but they tend to mean different things to different people and tend to refer to a range of specific behaviors, on the assumption that all these behaviors are part of the same thing. That assumption needs to be questioned at the beginning of the assessment process. The different behaviors being referred to may turn out to have different meanings. It is therefore more helpful at the beginning to identify behaviors like punching others, hitting head against solid objects, throwing furniture, screaming, taking other people's property rather than the more general terms identified above.

Starting with a specific list rather than more general terms makes it more likely that the assessment process will lead to a clear outcome. Listing the specifics also helps to stimulate the discussion about which issues justify outside intervention. Just because someone does something that other people dislike does not automatically justify professional intrusion and systematized attempts at change (see Chapter 1). An assessment effort should only be directed at behaviors that are justifiable targets.

When the list has been reduced to justifiable targets, it is legitimate to consider whether any of the specifics can be clustered together. This should only be done if two or more behaviors almost always occur together. If screaming is always accompanied by hitting and neither screaming nor hitting occur on their own, then they may be considered as a single unit. However, if screaming and hitting sometimes occur on their own it is wiser to consider them separately and to allow the assessment process to explore the links between them.

Prioritize

Once the list is finalized a decision will be needed as to which behavior(s) to prioritize for detailed assessment. Many people identified as challenging do several things that give rise to justifiable concerns. In most real world contexts limitations on resources mean that it will not be possible to do everything at once and everything that is required. To try to deal with everything may set the scene for confusion and ultimate failure in moving things forward. Such a failure in our efforts often gets projected onto the reputation of the person about whom we are concerned – *he* has failed, *he* is intractable, *he* does not respond to specific interventions and supports. This outcome is a disaster for the individual and his future prospects. It suggests that the behaviors are beyond influence and sets expectations that will turn into self-fulfilling prophecies. It is therefore important at the outset to prioritize the areas upon which we are going to focus and to acknowledge explicitly the issues that we are leaving for later. To pretend that we can do everything will be punishing for us and dangerous to the individual.

Once specific behaviors have been identified and priorities established, the assessment process can get under way. A framework is required to guide us in gathering and assembling the kind of information that is most likely to yield insight into why the behavior is occurring. Some of this information may already be available; some will need to be gathered specifically for the assessment.

A framework for analyzing human behavior

Exercise 3.1 An informal analysis of your own behavior

- Identify a behavior of your own that others might dislike, disapprove of, regard as socially or personally unacceptable (shouldn't be hard!).

- Think of some specific incidents of you behaving in this way.

- Imagine an alien who knew nothing of humankind but observed these incidents...and who was curious.

- Identify all the things that the alien would need to know in order to make some sense of that behavior – why that behavior, why then and in that situation and not at other times in other situations, why does it keep on happening every so often?

- List out these contributors and add up the number of things that you have identified.

Almost everyone will come up with more than one thing that the alien would need to know in order to make sense of the specific act – a simple but powerful reminder that behavior is rarely the result of a single cause. It is the result of several contributory factors that interact and accumulate to produce the outcome that we call 'an incident'. What will also probably have come out of the exercise is that the factors identified fall into a number of categories. Some have to do with the immediate situation (who said what to whom, what was going on at the time), some will be operating and often fluctuating over time (mood, stress level, relationship issues, life events, drug intake), some will reflect characteristics of the players (personality types, thinking styles). The understanding is not necessarily complex but it is certainly dynamic – factors will vary in their strength and significance over time and it may be only when a certain number of the contributors are 'aligned' that an incident occurs.

Thus the 'common sense' illustrated in Exercise 3.1 suggests we need to look in a number of different directions and use a number of different time frames for discovering the contributory factors that raise the likelihood of the specific behavior occurring.

Yet psychological theories do not make this easy to do. There are schools of thought that emphasize the roles of subsets of contributory factors, often disparaging the factors to which other theories draw attention. Behaviorists and psychoanalysts will expend considerable energy dismissing each other. In the real world of human behavior, no one school or branch of psychology has the answer – not social, developmental, cognitive, neuro, psychodynamic or behavioral. This 'common sense' point of view is well supported by a huge amount of scientific evidence. Any review of what we know about why humans engage in behaviors that cause serious concern in others concludes that such behaviors result from a messy interplay of multiple factors, biological and social, close in time and distant in time. Because this chapter is the intellectual heart of the book some sample references are included at the end to support the notion that 'common sense' and 'evidence based practice' are very close to each other in this respect.

Thus, if we are going to do a competent job at making sense of behavior we need a well-defined, broad-based framework that guides us through the assessment process in a way that makes it likely that we will identify as many of the contributory factors as possible. To access such a framework ordinary practitioners need a job aid that will help them to examine the factors that have been established empirically as influential in human behavior and that reflect the common sense made obvious in Exercise 3.1. At present there is no such agreed framework although a number of writers have made very significant attempts to broaden the base of our understanding (see the Acknowledgements, and the Resources list at the end of the book). Drawing upon this body of work the present chapter will try to identify the elements in such a framework, the bases that need to be covered and the areas about which information should be gathered. It is not proposed as a grand theory and it will not be presented in terms of a cute acronym. It is hoped that identifying the elements in the framework will be of some help to interested practitioners who may come from a variety of backgrounds. The elements will reflect the more empirical branches of psychology and what they have contributed to our understanding of human behavior. There is no suggestion that a contributory factor has to be found in every category for every behavior. Rather, when we are seeking to build an understanding of behavior we will need to gather information on all these areas and from that information extract the factors that appear to be contributing to the behavior of concern (see Chapter 5 for a more detailed discussion about this process of extraction).

The framework will be presented around the time frame over which factors operate:

- *Immediate* – for example, antecedents and consequences.

- *Short term* – for example, environmental conditions, social conditions, activities, mood state, physical state.

- *Longer term* – social system characteristics, quality of life, personality, current competences, physical or mental health issues, important past life events (loss, abuse or other traumas).

We will articulate the components in this chapter and then in the next chapter look at the tools that help us to gather quality information about each of these components.

Immediate factors

What happens immediately after a behavior can exert an important influence over whether that behavior occurs again. Insofar as behavior is followed by a change that is important to the individual, that satisfies some immediate want or need, then the behavior is more likely to be repeated in the future when similar circumstances arise. This is the process of reinforcement that can develop and sustain a behavior. Given that the behaviors with which this book is concerned are repeated, not isolated, occurrences, it is reasonable to assess whether there are events that follow the behavior that may be maintaining it. Such events are often put into two categories:

1.   The behavior may be followed by something occurring that satisfies some state of deprivation that the individual is experiencing – the behavior may lead to exciting sensory stimulation, access to previously unavailable goodies such as food, drinks, cigarettes, focal attention from other people, access to previously unavailable activities such as a walk. This is usually referred to as positive reinforcement.

2.   Alternatively the behavior may be sustained by negative reinforcement. The behavior is followed by the relief of some kind of aversive state – demands are withdrawn, space is cleared, pain goes away, noise reduces.

A behavior may be sustained by more than one type and category of reinforcement. The assessment of consequences is therefore an important element in building an understanding. Immediate consequences tend to be the most influential over behavior and consequences do not have to occur every time. Indeed once the behavior is established they may only occur rarely and still remain important influences. Thus it will be important to study many behavioral incidents before coming to any conclusion about possible reinforcement processes. This hunt will be made easier if we have information about the person's general preferences and things that are important in his life – the sorts of things that he generally strives to attain or avoid (see below). The maintaining consequences for the behaviors we identify as problematic tend not to be 'atypical' for the individual or accessed uniquely by the behavior of concern (an important issue to which we will return later).

Although an assessment must always include attention to reinforcement processes, not all behaviors are there because of reinforcement. Behaviors can occur because they are rule governed – the individual has developed an internal rule (often verbally encoded) that links the behavior to the situation ('This is what I do when...') irrespective of any consequence. It does not matter what happens after the behavior; it will continue to occur because that is the rule. We may sometimes characterize such behaviors as rituals or routines. A behavior may also be better characterized as occurring because of a loss of inhibitory control. The behavior is usually inhibited but in some circumstances (for example, under high levels of emotionality, following alcohol intake, when feeling tired or stressed) the inhibition fails and the behavior occurs but the consequences are irrelevant to any future occurrence. The key predictor of future occurrence is not the presence of a want or need but the functional capacity of the inhibitory system. This is complicated because the behavior usually occurs in response to some immediate issue. However, the individual will normally deal with that issue in a different way (will talk about the problem, will walk away from the situation), rather than, for example, lashing out. It is only when the issue arises and inhibitory control is reduced that the outburst occurs. The issue of inhibition can be more relevant than the issue of reinforcement. Some of the indicators that inhibition is the key issue are the links between incidents and arousal level (incidents only occurring if arousal escalates beyond a certain threshold), signs of active attempts to stop the behavior (for example, sitting on hands, asking others to move away) and evidence of genuine remorse or distress following an incident.

The second type of immediate contributor is events occurring just before the behavior of concern – sometimes referred to as antecedents or triggers. Such events may serve one or two functions. They may be purely informational events (discriminative stimuli):

> *I want a cigarette but there is no point hassling people who do not smoke and do not carry cigarettes but as soon as the smoker appears the behavior starts.*

Such events may also be motivational (establishing operations):

> *I was doing fine until that person stepped into my space and started hassling me to do that task and then I experienced an overwhelming need to be left alone.*

Discrete events that occur before a behavior are relatively easy to spot. However, it will again be important to know about the individual's general preferences and sensitivities as we may fail to spot events that do not seem significant in our personal worlds. It is only the person who is deeply emotionally engaged by dogs, lawn mowers, earthmovers and road sweepers who will notice the noise arising from these sources. It is only the person who cannot sort stimuli by relevance who will become distressed by a situation occurring elsewhere that we do not think involves her (for example, somebody talking in the next room). Perhaps the most difficult establishing operations to spot are those that are based upon events not happening:

> *It is only when I have not received some kind of social acknowledgement or some kind of sensory excitement in the last 7.5 minutes that I reach the point of trying to resolve this preference of mine.*

Some behaviors are triggered by such absences and the time parameters can be quite specific and difficult to spot in real world situations. Finally some of the antecedents may be internal and therefore not accessible to direct observation – the sudden twinge, the sudden thought, the flashback, the heart flutter, the voice speaking to us. We normally start to look for these events by default when we have failed to find any other antecedents, and such episodes may be described as 'coming out of the blue'. Occasionally we may be able to access them by other observational methods (for example, psychophysiological measures). More often we may 'hypothesize' their presence based upon consideration of all that we know about the individual (for example, her physical or mental health status, her history). We should certainly not 'hypothesize out of the blue' by suggesting an antecedent on the basis of nothing that is known about the person. Better to say 'unknown' if we have failed to observe an antecedent and no other information suggests a plausible, internal possibility.

Short term

The next area of assessment is events occurring before the behavior but that are not necessarily immediate antecedents. These are ongoing situations that tend to be associated with the behavior occurring. They are measured in minutes and hours rather than days or weeks. Their role may be directly motivational; they generate the wants or needs that the individual will act to deal with – they are in that sense like the antecedent establishing operations. They may also contribute to escalating arousal and increasing the likelihood of loss of inhibitory control. They are sometimes referred to as setting conditions or ecological conditions. They can be divided into two categories:

1.   Characteristics of the external environment

2.   Characteristics of the internal environment.

EXTERNAL ENVIRONMENTAL FACTORS

- Physical – for example, noise levels, lighting conditions, temperature, aroma, space available.

- Activational – the activities available to engage with (or not).

- Organizational – the extent to which a situation is organized so that everybody knows what the situation is about and what they are to do in that situation, whether the situation has some specific purpose or not (we sometimes use the notion of structure – is the situation structured or unstructured?).

- Social – who is around and what is their availability (for example, staff handover times, activity transitions involving tidying and setting up)?

- Temporal – a transition when one activity is ending and another is about to begin; time of day, perhaps linking to individual biorhythms (early morning, after lunch, late afternoon).

This takes us into those conditions that may be part of the individual's internal environment.

INTERNAL ENVIRONMENTAL FACTORS

- Individual biorhythms and energy level – people vary in when they are most alert and energetic in a day and incidents may cluster around the highs or lows of individual biorhythms.

- Emotional states – transient moods involving tension, anxiety, anger, excitement, sadness.

- Physical states – ongoing discomforts such as blocked sinus, headache, full bowel.

These are all areas that an assessment process will need to cover to see if there are contributory factors that are setting the scene for behaviors to occur even if they do not trigger incidents directly.

Longer term

Behavior is influenced by certain longer-term environmental and personal characteristics. These include:

1. Social system characteristics

2. Quality of life

3. Personality

4. Current competences

5. Physical health issues

6. Mental health issues

7. Life events.

SOCIAL SYSTEM CHARACTERISTICS

There are a number of ways in which social systems operate that raise the likelihood of members of that system acting out:

(a) People find it harder to function when they are embedded in a social system marked by high levels of conflict – where participants actively and overtly disagree with each other and fail to resolve these disagreements. Such conflicted systems may impact upon motivation – they generate uncomfortable feelings from which relief is needed. They can model various forms of aggression. They may also impact upon reinforcement processes so that the behaviors of concern are not responded to consistently – some members of the social system reinforce them and others do not, thus establishing reinforcement schedules associated with sustaining the behavior in question.

(b) High expressed emotion is another important social system characteristic. A highly emotional atmosphere, particularly if it involves frequent criticism of the individual, may collapse the individual's well-being and raise the likelihood of behaviors that others will find unacceptable.

(c)   Power distribution is also an issue to consider. If the person is embedded in a social system in which she has very little influence or control, she may fight for some control or give up in despair. Either outcome may be associated with behaviors that will raise concern. Alternatively, if the individual is embedded in a system in which she has absolute control and no limits are set and no one else is permitted to have a say, then again the individual's behavior can become very dangerous to others.

(d)   The final important social system characteristic is the extensiveness and overall quality of the individual's social network. Humans cannot function in isolation – we are an inextricably interdependent animal. Isolate the human from social support and the immune system malfunctions, mood declines, problem solving abilities decline and 'strange ideas' develop. All these factors may be associated with overt behaviors that give rise to concern. We are all dependent on having a number of people around us to whom we can relate positively and who think well of us. Without that kind of support any individual is at considerable risk for impaired social functioning.

Thus part of a comprehensive assessment will involve assessing the social systems in which the individual is embedded. It will also involve looking at other 'quality of life' indices.

QUALITY OF LIFE

Important components of life quality are the quality of housing, the range and quality of activities, the diversity of roles that the individual experiences, the pace of life, the income level. We can use objective indicators and normative standards ('compared with other people of a similar age in this society...') but we must also include personal satisfaction – the extent to which any of these quality of life indicators are important to the individual. The concept of niche is very important – is the individual in the kind of life that works well for him? Insofar as people are not leading the lives that work for them as individuals then the lack of satisfaction and stress that this involves may well be reflected in their behavior.

There are then longer-term personal characteristics that will inform our understanding of why certain behaviors are occurring.

PERSONALITY

This refers to characteristics of the individual that inform us about enduring motivations, tendencies and dispositions. Extroverts tend to like a lot of social interactions and seek those out; introverts may avoid too much social contact. Those who are anxious may have a number of specific worries and situations they avoid and may easily become anxious in new/uncertain situations or find it hard to cope with too much stimulation. Thrill seekers may get bored easily and require high levels of stimulation in order to feel comfortable. Some people are eager to please others even at expense to themselves; some are much more driven to please themselves even at the expense of others. Control freaks are very uncomfortable in situations where others determine what goes on; mellow fellows are troubled less by such situations. The professional labels that surround people regarded as disabled often overshadow these key aspects of any human being. Yet the motivations underlying behaviors that give rise to concern often reflect these enduring personal characteristics rather than more transient but universal motivations such as hunger, thirst or sex.

CURRENT COMPETENCES

Personal competence also relates to behavioral issues. There are five key areas of competence that relate particularly to socially challenging behavior:

(a)   Communication skills. If a person cannot express important needs and preferences in a way that others can understand, she has to find a way of getting the message across, a way that makes others pay close attention, right now. If she cannot understand what others are communicating, she may feel very confused about what is going on, be unable to predict what is going to happen and not know how to function appropriately in the situation.

(b)   Social knowledge and understanding. Insofar as an individual understands and regards as important the effect that his behavior has on others, the effect it has on how they will think about him and the longer-term social consequences, he may well inhibit impulses to take direct action when angry, upset or in other ways needy. If he lacks this competence, he will be much more likely to act as he feels when he feels it, no holds barred.

(c)   The ability to register and manage arousal and mood states. Insofar as someone is unable to analyze these emotional variables or does not know how to self-manage them in constructive ways, then that individual will be vulnerable to becoming overwhelmed and losing control.

(d)   Flexible thinking. If a person tends to get stuck on topics and cannot move on to thinking about other things (perseveration) then she may upset other people and their reaction may set off an escalation sequence that results in an 'incident'. If the thing that she dwells on is a source of upset (for example, a negative memory) then she will become trapped in a negative and escalating state that at some point will be acted out.

(e)   The ability to think of things to do and do them – self-occupation competence. Without self-occupation skills, people are very dependent upon others to find things for them to do and help them to do the activities. In the real world this means that people without self-occupation competence are very vulnerable to experiencing boredom and seeking stimulation that relieves that state…and stimulus seeking may be regarded by others as challenging, especially if the individual is by temperament a thrill seeker!

PHYSICAL HEALTH ISSUES

These include the sorts of general physical health issues that can affect anyone (minor to major) at any time. In addition, some people have chronic or recurring conditions that will impact upon their well-being and motivations – joint pain, sinus infection and allergies, bowel problems. If a person is in continual pain and discomfort it may directly impact behavior – for example, leading to self-injury that may distract from the physical pain and more directly relieve it by releasing endogenous opiates. Health issues can also impact indirectly by reducing tolerance to everyday stressors. The notion of health is often now extended to include the notion of mental health.

MENTAL HEALTH ISSUES

Some of the phenomena that lead to the ascription of psychiatric classificatory labels will relate to overt behaviors that give rise to concern. Thus extended phases of low mood (depression) may lead to behaviors that get rid of demands and other social intrusions or that relieve the physical pain that people can experience. Extended elevations of mood may disinhibit behaviors directly, impair social judgment and increase the need for intense stimulation. Some people may be troubled by the voices they hear and either try to drown out the voices or do as the voices tell them. The resulting behaviors may be challenging to others. Some people may develop beliefs that others mean harm to them, beliefs that are strong but not shared by anyone else. If they believe themselves to be at risk they may well do things that are dangerous for others.

LIFE EVENTS

How someone is now may reflect what has gone on before. Single, discrete life events such as bereavement or being a victim of crime may impact the individual's well-being long after the event itself – even worse if there has been repeated experience of such trauma, as is often the case for those who have been physically or sexually abused.

Although daily hassles – demand overload, things not going to plan – are not as deeply significant from a psychological point of view they may still impact upon overt behavior. Thus if someone is going through a lot of changes or disruptions of routines she may well become more stressed and irritable and show this through behavior.

Finally it will be important to consider the role models to which a person has been exposed. The behaviors that concern us now may well be the behaviors that the individual has seen a significant person engage in. Exposure to a physically or sexually violent parent may develop a template about how relationships are to be conducted and this template may be what we are seeing in the current behavioral concern.

Thus building our understanding of a behavior needs to consider all these possible factors. We work out from the immediate contributors along a time line, in the fashion of Russian dolls, by starting to look at the smallest (most immediate) which is then placed inside the next one up and so on. There are not necessarily factors at every level and we will not always have enough information to establish whether a contributor is present (we may not know someone's history, we may not know enough about some of the social dynamics, we may not be able to access someone's internal experiences). Nevertheless if we take an approach that works systematically through the possibilities we are more likely to develop a quality understanding of what is going on and we will also open up a number of possible avenues of help, things that we can do that will make the situation better.

Protective resources

It will also help if we include in our assessment work an itemization of the protective resources that the individual has. Thus far we have emphasized the problematic behaviors and the vulnerability factors that contribute to these behaviors. We will be looking to intervene to remedy those factors, to enhance and enrich the individual's resources. This process will be helped if we can identify some of the positive resources that the individual brings to the table.

We will consider three key areas:

1. *Social support.* We should identify who is in the person's support network that thinks well of the individual and/or is keen to offer help.

2. *Successful spaces.* We should identify the situations in which the behavior of concern never occurs or is very unlikely to occur. This may be certain places, activities, and times of day,

the company of certain people or particular periods in a person's life.

3. *Personal capacities.* We should identify in some detail examples of the person successfully communicating a need or preference, successfully coping with an emotional or mood state, being able to shift thinking, successfully occupying themselves or showing some awareness of the needs of others. Even though people may have major difficulties in these areas, difficulties that contribute to the behaviors of concern, when we look closely there are often examples of competence. It is a lot easier to build on a competence already present than to teach a whole new one.

Concluding remarks

This chapter has tried to indicate the areas that an assessment should cover if we are to raise the likelihood of developing a useful understanding of why a behavior occurs. These areas are summarized in Table 3.1. It has been about the *what* of assessment. In the next chapter we go on to consider the *how* – what methods of assessment can help us to assemble quality information in each of the areas identified as relevant.

Table 3.1: Assessment areas	
Immediate factors	**Short-term factors**
Consequences Positive reinforcement Negative reinforcement Loss of inhibition/control	**External environmental factors** Physical Activational Organizational Social Temporal
Antecedents/triggers Information events Motivation events Arousal induction events	**Internal environmental factors** Individual biorhythms and energy level Emotional states Physical states
Longer-term factors	**Protective resources**
Social system characteristics Quality of life Personality Current competences Physical health issues Mental health issues Life events	Social support Successful spaces Personal capacities

Bibliography

Bronfenbrenner, U. (1977) 'Toward an Experimental Ecology of Human Development.' *American Psychologist 32*, 513–531.

Clements, J. (1992) 'I Can't Explain…Challenging Behaviour: Towards a Shared, Conceptual Framework.' *Clinical Psychology Forum 39*, 29–37.

Donnellan, A., LaVigna, G.W., Negri-Shoultz, N. and Sassbender, L.L. (1988) *Progress Without Punishment: Effective Approaches for Learners with Behavior Problems.* New York: Teachers College Press.

Dykens, E.M. (2000) 'Psychopathology in Children with Intellectual Disability'. *Journal of Child Psychology and Psychiatry 41*, 4, 407–418.

Emerson, E., Hatton, C., Bromley, J. and Caine, A. (1998) *Clinical Psychology and People with Intellectual Disabilities.* Chichester: Wiley.

Hill, J. (2002) 'Biological, psychological and social processes in the conduct disorders.' *Journal of Child Psychology and Psychiatry 43*, 1, 133–164.

Leff, J. and Vaughn, C.E. (1985) *Expressed Emotion in Families: Its Significance for Mental Illness.* New York: Guilford Press.

O'Hara, J. and Sperlinger, A. (1997) *Adults with Learning Disabilities: A Practical Approach for Health Professionals.* Chichester: Wiley.

Pfadt, A. (1997) 'Multiple Perspectives on People with Challenging Behavior: A Framework for Changing Approaches'. *The Habilitative Mental Healthcare Newsletter 16*, 4, 69–72.

Rutter, M. (2000) 'Psychosocial Influences: Critiques, Findings and Research Tools.' *Development and Psychopathology 12*, 375–406.

Zarkowska, E. and Clements, J. (1994) *Problem Behaviour and People with Severe Learning Disabilities: The STAR Approach.* London: Chapman & Hall.

CHAPTER 4

The Tool Box

John Clements and Neil Martin

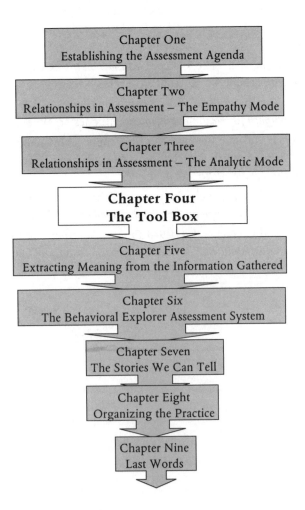

Chapter One
Establishing the Assessment Agenda

Chapter Two
Relationships in Assessment – The Empathy Mode

Chapter Three
Relationships in Assessment – The Analytic Mode

**Chapter Four
The Tool Box**

Chapter Five
Extracting Meaning from the Information Gathered

Chapter Six
The Behavioral Explorer Assessment System

Chapter Seven
The Stories We Can Tell

Chapter Eight
Organizing the Practice

Chapter Nine
Last Words

This chapter will look at how to focus an assessment and gather information so that the reasons for a behavior are likely to be clarified. Searching for reasons means knowing where to look. Whilst that sounds obvious, there are many different theories about human behavior. These theories can differ greatly in where they point us for answers and in what they regard as the most important information to gather. A psychoanalytic perspective would urge us to learn as much as we can about the person's early experiences – to go back in time. An operant behavioral perspective would urge us to learn as much as we can about the immediate circumstances that surround incidents of behavior – to focus on the now. We all carry in our heads theories and explanations about why people do what they do. Sometimes these are everyday, 'common sense' theories; sometimes they are theories that we have been formally taught. Sometimes we are consciously aware of our theories, sometimes not. And, of course, we all tend to seek information that supports the theories that we already hold – no one likes to be challenged, let alone be wrong!

Chapter 3 presented a framework to guide the process of information gathering. The framework was drawn from both common sense and the more empirical branches of psychology. There is no suggestion that it is somehow 'right'. It is a guide. It is based upon the assumption that we are more likely to find out why a behavior occurs if we have a systematic way of analyzing potential contributors than if we hope that the answer will somehow make itself evident to us as we take a haphazard walk through the available information or rely on our gut feelings and intuitions.

If we accept the usefulness of having a structured framework the question then moves on to how such information should be gathered. We need information that has a degree of solidity (reliability and validity, as some would say). The same information overall should emerge whether we gather it on a Tuesday or a Wednesday. The same information should emerge whether I or a colleague gather the information. The same information should emerge whether I observe the behavior directly or ask someone who knows the person and the behavior. However, all methods of gathering information are error prone. There is no 'gold standard'. Direct observation is not necessarily better than talking to people who know the person and the situation well. Filling out charts is not necessarily superior to completing a questionnaire. Statistical analysis is not necessarily superior to qualitative interpretation. All methods have their pitfalls and some of the common ones are discussed in the next section. We need to be mindful of these and to take steps to avoid errors as much as we can. In real world service settings we will be limited in our options compared with more academic, research oriented settings. In research settings it may be possible to have two different people collecting the same information to see if they come up with the same results, to collect the same information twice over, on separate occasions, to have two separate people look at the same data to see if they draw the same conclusions. These formal methods of 'reliability' checking will rarely be feasible in ordinary service settings.

Whilst the solidity of information is important there is a very real and practical check on what we are doing. At some point information has to be summarized into a working theory (see Chapter 5). From this theory real world interventions will be derived. The bottom line becomes whether the person's life quality, satisfaction, well-being and behavioral functioning change following implementation of the planned interventions. If not, then one possibility is that the information on which the interventions were based was not solid enough and needs to be revisited. There are of course other possible explanations (for example, poor implementation of the interventions, lack of time for effects to show, insensitive monitoring systems, faulty interpretation of monitoring data). However, being anchored to real outcomes for real people provides a means of regularly considering and reconsidering the quality of the information available. It is clearly preferable that the initial assessment information is as solid as possible. This will reduce a source of error. More importantly it will fulfill our professional duty to serve and support the individual in the most effective and efficient way possible. It is simply not appropriate to waste the time of the individual and the resources allocated to her support services by sloppy initial assessment work that leads to inept interventions. The behavioral bottom line thus provides an additional safeguard.

There are two main ways in which assessment information is gathered. We may talk to the person and those who know him and the situation well, either directly (interviewing) or indirectly (checklists and questionnaires). We may observe the person as he goes about his everyday life and record information about behavior and circumstances. In the next section we look briefly at some of the common problems with these general methods of assessment. We then go on to look at some of the options for gathering the specific information that we have identified as appropriate, using the framework that we adopted in Chapter 3.

Some general difficulties with information gathering

Conversations with others

INTERVIEWING

Much information will be gathered by talking to people – the person whose behavior is of concern and those who know/have known that person. Getting solid information from discussions and interviews depends upon a number of factors. Such talks are more likely to be productive if the person gathering the information is clear about what information she is after. Thus a structured, organized protocol will be better than a general 'chat'. The person from whom information is being gathered must have access to the information. Sounds obvious but, in practice, service protocol and family culture may lead to information being provided by the person who knows least. In hierarchical services, an outside assessor may be directed to talk to supervisors or managers, the people who are supposed to 'know' but may in reality have very limited contact with the person, far less than 'lower status' staff who are with the person day in, day out. In certain cultural contexts it will be required that the father is the provider of information even though he may have very limited day-to-day involvement with his son or daughter. Thus the requirement of a 'knowledgeable informant' is not always easy to meet.

The way in which a discussion is conducted will also influence the quality of the information provided. The notion of rapport is important – those involved in the discussion have to feel comfortable with each other. Thus an interviewer has to be able to put people at their ease, to reduce any sense of power differences both by social skills and by environmental arrangements such as seating. 'Demand characteristics' are important. These discussions are about drawing from people what they know. If people feel that they will be criticized for admitting to certain things, including not knowing, then the information provided will be distorted. If the interview is conducted as a test, again people will be looking to provide the 'right' answers, the answers that they think the interviewer wants to hear, rather than the most accurate answers. Questioning style plays a role – leading questions and too many closed questions (those with a yes/no answer) will distort the information flow. The use of open questions to draw people out followed up with specific questions is a strategy more likely to yield solid information. Anyone who gathers information by talking to other people would be well advised to get training in interviewing.

Thus gathering information by talking to people will be more likely to yield solid results if there is a structured protocol in the hands of a skilled interviewer. Readers will only have to reflect on their experiences of meetings about behavior to know how rarely such basic requirements are met.

QUESTIONNAIRES

One particular version of interviewing is use of a questionnaire. As with interviewing, there are whole books written about questionnaire design. Readers who want to design their own questionnaires would be advised to get familiar with the basics of design. Again, the need for knowledgeable informants is important. The design of the questions needs to emphasize things that people know and/or have observed rather than encouraging them to speculate on what might be the case. The answer format needs to be careful not to encourage 'response sets' – if too many consecutive answers are 'yes' on a 'yes/no' questionnaire then there will be a tendency to keep checking 'yes'. If people are being encouraged to provide numerical ratings, going above nine points on a scale is unlikely to be useful.

Observation and recording

The other major approach to gathering information is to observe the person going about his everyday life and to record what has been observed. Observation is sometimes thought to be superior to other forms of information gathering but it has its own problems. The very presence of someone observing and/or recording alters the situation – the individual's behavior may change in response to this change in the environment (reactivity). This effect often decreases in time but some people may be generally very disturbed by this sort of scrutiny. The second problem is the skill of the observer. The question of 'demand characteristics' is again relevant. If the observer has already made up his mind about what the facts of the matter are then it is likely that he will observe and record only those things that fit the preconceptions. A good observer has to be open-minded. Given that all observation is selective a good observer has to learn to process as much information as possible, with as little screening for (assumed) relevance as possible. This takes practice! The process can be greatly facilitated if there is the option of making some permanent audio/video record so that the situation can be gone over repeatedly.

Given limitations on processing capacity even the most open-minded observer has to know generally what to focus upon. As with conversational methods, one can observe in an unstructured way, trying to remain as open as possible to what is going on and hoping that relevant connections will emerge. Alternatively one can use a more structured approach and gather information in terms of well-defined categories. Ideally one should do both – start with unstructured observation and use that to develop a more structured, categorical approach, which is more likely to yield solid information.

In practice direct observation often involves observing at particular times and in particular circumstances. It involves sampling. This raises the question as to whether the sample will be representative enough to yield solid information (generalizable conclusions) about the influences over the individual's behavior.

The ways in which observations are recorded will also impact the solidity of the information gathered. The closer in time that recording is to observation, the less the likelihood of loss or distortion through memory. The system of recording will be important. Long-hand writing or writing notes is time consuming and distracts from observation. However, it may be the best way if little is known about the situation and we are at the earliest stages of gathering information (see above). As we develop our understanding, use of structured category systems may speed the recording, reduce distraction from observation itself and make it easier to spot patterns of association. This is true whether one is using paper and pencil or computer assisted methods.

Thus an open-minded, skilled observer with a well-organized and practiced recording system will generate more solid information than someone untrained in observation filling out a diary at the end of the day. Again, readers will reflect on how often these conditions are met in ordinary service practice. It certainly raises an important and much neglected area of training, particularly for paid staff, and raises issues about the tools that we provide to staff. It is hoped that this volume will make a contribution in both areas.

Some tools for the trade

Identifying the behavior of concern

An assessment needs to be focused around a specific, well-defined behavior. Identifying this focus will often be done by discussions between all those involved, including the person himself. This may be relatively straightforward. However, some people will present with multiple concerns and it may take time to reach agreement on priorities. Those involved may differ in what they consider most in need of attention – behaviors impact differently upon different people. Those involved may vary a lot in the experience that they have in working with behavioral issues and some behaviors will have a much greater impact in some environments than others (screaming might make a relatively small impact in a remote institution but a huge impact if you are living in a house with neighbors close on either side). It is important to allow for time in deciding priorities. If one powerful group member makes all the decisions but is dependent upon the others for gathering assessment information, then the quality of assessment information will be impacted. If others do not feel committed to working on a particular issue or have other urgent concerns that they feel are being neglected, this is likely to reduce the quality of their contribution to the assessment process.

To assist the process of defining and prioritizing behaviors some people may want to use one of the published scales that rate the sorts of behavior difficulties that give rise to concern in those who support people with developmental disabilities. Some of these are listed in Table 4.1. These can be useful in facilitating discussions about priorities and defusing personal conflicts. Many of these scales also generate numerical scores that may have some small value in assessing progress, comparing scores before and after support plans are put in place. The problem with them as measures of progress is that they tend to be relatively insensitive and will only reflect very large and enduring changes – much behavioral work is about smaller changes, growing over time but often running a fluctuating course. Changes that are individually and socially significant may not be detected by these rating scales.

Table 4:1: Some published scales for rating behavior difficulties
Aberrant Behavior Checklist
Reiss Screen for Maladaptive Behavior
AAMR Adaptive Behavior Scale, Part 2
Vineland Adaptive Behavior Scale, Part 2
Child Behavior Checklist
Behavioral and Emotional Rating Scale

Once a focus is agreed upon, information is needed about the possible contributory factors. In Chapter 3 we identified a 'time of operation' framework and the first two categories were immediate and short term. We will consider these two categories together.

Assessing immediate and short-term contributory factors

The sorts of influences that we identified in these categories were antecedents and consequences and various characteristics of the external and internal environment (see Table 4.2, drawn from Chapter 3).

Table 4.2: Short-term influences over behavior

External environmental factors

Physical – for example, noise levels, lighting conditions, temperature, aroma, space available.

Activational – the activities available to engage with (or not).

Organizational – the extent to which a situation is organized so that everybody knows what the situation is about and what they are to do in that situation, whether the situation has some specific purpose or not (we sometimes use the notion of structure – is the situation structured or unstructured?).

Social – who is around and what is their availability (for example, staff handover times, activity transitions involving tidying and setting up)?

Temporal – a transition when one activity is ending and another is about to begin; time of day, perhaps linking to individual biorhythms (early morning, after lunch, late afternoon).

Internal environmental factors

Individual biorhythms and energy level – people vary in when they are most alert and energetic in a day and incidents may cluster around the highs or lows of individual biorhythms.

Emotional states – transient moods involving tension, anxiety, anger, excitement, sadness.

Physical states – ongoing discomforts such as blocked sinus, headache, full bowel.

PARTICIPANT OBSERVATION AND RECORDING

The most common approach to assessing such factors is for those who support the person on a day-to-day basis (family members, teachers, job coaches, residential workers) to make a record whenever an incident occurs. A record is made of what the person actually did and details of the immediate circumstances. This may be done in the form of a diary or using a specific incident recording form. One such common form used to be the A-B-C chart, laid out in three columns, one marked **A**ntecedents, one marked **B**ehavior, and one marked **C**onsequences. In view of the comments above, a more structured format for gathering information raises the likelihood of the information being solid. Figure 4.1 illustrates a more detailed recording form that guides the observer to record under key headings and also offers the opportunity to use check boxes. This form encourages the separation (literally) of fact from interpretation. Assessment involves keeping these records and at some point analyzing them. Important contributors will not be obvious from each individual record so that a number of records will need to be analyzed for recurring themes, factors that appear often in the recordings. As a rule of thumb, such an analysis is particularly difficult with less than 20 separate recordings.

It is not always clear exactly how to analyze a collection of such charts and the data that they contain. By looking through them a skilled interpreter may be able to 'see' a pattern (the eyeball technique!). Appendix 1 offers a guide for carrying out this process a little more systematically. This is only a crude guide as there are many pitfalls in making sense of incident records. For example, the fact that 90 percent of incident records indicate that the environment was noisy at the time of an incident might suggest noise as a contributor. However, if the person spends 90 percent of her life in a noisy environment then you would expect that to show on 90 percent of the records even if noise made no contribution. That would be the level of association by chance. This issue of 'base rates' is very hard to resolve in practical settings so that Appendix 1 should be seen as no more than a job aid that assists with the development of hypotheses. A final practical note is that such detailed recordings will usually only be feasible with relatively

BEHAVIORAL EXPLORER – INCIDENT RECORDING FORM

NAME:

BEHAVIOR TO BE TRACKED:

Tick each applicable statement and/or write information in your own words

WHAT HAPPENED IMMEDIATELY AFTER THE INCIDENT
(consequences/results)

Given food, drink or a cigarette [ ] Received more social contact/attention [ ]
Received less social contact/attention [ ] Went to quieter area (fewer people around) [ ]
Given a task/activity [ ] Had sensory stimulation (previously unavailable) [ ]
Demands or requests withdrawn/reduced [ ] Given more help to complete task/activity[ ]
Taken out for a walk [ ] 'Counseled' about behavior [ ] Sensory input reduced [ ]
Other (please specify) [ ]

WHAT HAPPENED JUST BEFORE THE INCIDENT (antecedents/triggers)

Food or drink present or being prepared [ ] Asked to do something [ ]
Particular individual present/entered the room [ ]
Told that s/he couldn't have or do something [ ]
No social contact/attention for several mins. [ ]
No involvement in task/activity for several mins. [ ]
Target of teasing or verbal abuse [ ] Involved in an argument [ ]
Occurrence of 'sensitive' event [ ] Other (please specify) [ ]

THE SITUATION IN WHICH INCIDENT TOOK PLACE (setting conditions)

PHYSICAL ENVIRONMENT:
Quiet [ ] Noisy [ ] Hot [ ] Cold [ ] Other (please specify) [ ]

SOCIAL ENVIRONMENT:
Alone [ ] Crowded [ ] Arguments going on [ ] Other (please specify) [ ]

PERSONAL STATE:
In pain/discomfort [ ] Angry [ ] Tense [ ] Excited [ ] Happy [ ] Tired [ ]
Other (please specify) [ ]

EVENTS OF THE PREVIOUS 3 HOURS:
Arguments [ ] Disruption of routine [ ] Family visits [ ] Other (please specify)

YOUR FEELINGS ABOUT THE INCIDENT

HOW THE BEHAVIOR MADE YOU FEEL:

WHAT YOU THOUGHT THE INCIDENT WAS ABOUT:

SIGNED: NAME (printed):   TIME OF INCIDENT: DATE:

Figure 4.1: Example of detailed incident recording form

infrequent incidents (perhaps three to six a day maximum). For higher frequency behaviors, simpler formats will be needed.

One such option is the scatterplot that combines ease of recording with built in visual analysis (in most service settings analysis and interpretation will be through some variation of the eyeball approach). This is illustrated in Figure 4.2. The columns represent days (the example shows a chart to cover a one-month period). The rows represent time of day/activities. Specific behavior codes are entered in the cells. In addition important events (for example, family visits, a bout of illness, a change in medication, arrival of a new person) can be marked in on the day that they occur. Whilst such an assessment does not give detailed information on antecedents and consequences it does indicate relationships between behavior and time of day, activities engaged in and life events. It is relatively simple to complete and reduces the role of the personal interpretation of the person completing the recording. The example in Figure 4.2 clearly illustrates associations of behavior with time of day. Further investigation would be needed to amplify the interpretation, to tease out if it is to do with activities, transitions or mood state or something else that goes on at those times.

As well as the recording format there is an issue about giving people a time and decision making frame for this work. People generally deliver better quality recording if they know for how long they are being asked to do it. It works better to tell people that 'We will do this for a week/month/three months…and then summarize what we have learned and put some plans in place', rather than setting a system up without it being clear what the end point is and what will be done with the information collected.

There are therefore a number of options to choose from if our approach to assessment is going to involve asking those who support the person to keep some kind of record of their observations when incidents of the behavior occur. Good practice involves:

- using a structured recording format rather than an unstructured one

- choosing a format that is feasible to implement, bearing in mind the frequency of incidents

NAME: Ryan
DATE: May

BEHAVIOR CODES AND INSTRUCTIONS

P pushing others **S** screaming for more than 2 seconds
H hit self **B** biting or trying to bite others

Whenever one of the above behaviors occurs, mark the letter codes in time period in which the incident occurred

	1	2	3	4	5	6	7	8	9	10	11	12	13	14	15	16	17	18	19	20	21	22	23	24	25	26	27	28	29	30	31
6–8			P							P				P	P							P		P						P	P
8–10																															
10–12						SS															S								SH		
12–2																		B													
2–4																															
4–6	SS S HH		SS S			S HH H	SS		SS S HH	SS S			SS		S H	SS S SS		SS S	SS S H	S	SS S S	SS H	SS				SS		SS S S HH H		
6–8			P							P												P					P				
8–10																															
night																															

Figure 4.2: Example of scatterplot form

- training those who will use the recording system both in terms of how to fill in the chart and in keeping the focus on facts, not interpretations
- setting a time frame for the assessment process
- making sure that the information collected is analyzed and that the results are fed back to those who have collected it so that there is appreciation expressed for them having collected the information
- using other ways to gather the same information to see if similar results emerge (see next sections).

INTERVIEWS AND QUESTIONNAIRES

Information about the immediate and short-term influences can also be gathered by someone interviewing those people who are with the individual on a day-to-day basis and drawing from them what they have learned by being with the person. A shortened way of interviewing to draw out people's knowledge is to give them a questionnaire. The Behavioral Explorer detailed in Chapter 6 can be used as an interview format and Appendix 2 presents another option for this type of assessment (see also O'Neill *et al.* 1997). As already mentioned interviews are more likely to yield solid information if:

- a structured format is used
- the interviewer is skilled
- the persons being interviewed are knowledgeable
- the focus (for present purposes) is on what has been observed (not on beliefs or opinions) about the areas detailed in Figure 4.1.

The interview does have some advantages over incident recording. It is easier sometimes to get people to tell you what they know than it is to get them to keep records. Keeping records is a notoriously difficult enterprise in most practical settings – they may not get kept, those kept may get lost, what is recorded is very variable in quality. It is possible to get a rich array of solid quantitative and qualitative information from a well-organized and well-administered interview. The conditions outlined above may not always be met in practice but certainly assessment by interview should not be regarded as 'second best' compared with participant observation and recording.

Questionnaires are less used in assessment work. The best known is the Motivation Assessment Scale, devised by Durand and Crimmins (reproduced in O'Neill *et al.* 1997). This draws from people what they have learned about the immediate circumstances (antecedents and consequences) most associated with the behavior of concern. It focuses around four categories of behavior-reinforcement relationship (behavior as attention getting, demand escaping, self-stimulatory or materially rewarded). It is therefore very limited in scope and doubts have been raised about the solidity of the information gained in this way. It is, however, easy to complete and it can be interesting to give it independently to several people involved in the individual's life and then feed back the results. Sometimes this shows that people see things very differently; sometimes it shows that although people talk in different ways about the individual they actually see the same things. People come to realize that the way they have been interpreting the person's behavior is wrong; the behavior is really about something else and this kind of insight is a more effective way of shifting beliefs than trying to persuade someone by talking at them. So, for a number of reasons a questionnaire like the Motivation Assessment Scale can be considered as part of the assessment process, in combination with other approaches such as participant observation and recording or a structured interview.

A questionnaire type exercise sometimes used by the author when carrying out an assessment is the 'three questions exercise'. This is a quick way of getting a number of potentially useful items of information.

Question 1: What are the circumstances most and least likely to be associated with the behavior in question?
This is laid out as two columns on a piece of paper and people put what they know in each column. This is an attempt to get at some of the other shorter-term factors that are missed by the Motivation Assessment Scale. It looks at those factors associated with incidents but also at those factors that currently associate with constructive functioning (when the

behavior is least likely to occur). This opens up additional possibilities for helping the person by building on her successes. Also, by entering the factors together, it sometimes shows linkages and causes that may not be obvious if you only focus on the factors associated with incidents being most likely to occur, which is what most assessment approaches focus upon.

Question 2: Day from heaven, day from hell
Again this is done on a piece of paper divided into two columns. Those doing the exercise are asked to imagine that they are freed from all constraints and have unlimited resources. They are then asked to think about what they would do to create a day for the person that would make it very unlikely that the behavior in question would occur at all (day from heaven). This is then turned around to what they would do to create a day when the behavior would occur very often (day from hell). There is a lot of overlap with Question 1 but Question 2 draws from people the particular things that they can do that make a difference. This is important because often by the time that an individual's behavior is being raised publicly as of concern, those working with the person are beginning to feel hopeless. They have already tried a lot and feel that nothing has worked; they are starting to talk about incidents coming 'out of the blue' and occurring 'for no good reason' and to attribute the influences to processes internal to the individual. Sometimes this may be true but often it reflects frustration around the real world constraints under which people are operating. They have limited resources and often carry responsibilities towards people other than just the individual. Question 2 is a way of reminding people that they do know something about the behavior in question and can do things that make a difference, even if practical constraints make it hard sometimes to avoid triggering incidents and to support positive functioning.

Question 3: If the behavior ceased, what image do you have of what the person would be doing instead in those situations in which the problematic behavior currently occurs?
This is the old behavioral question that helps people to focus on the alternative skills and behaviors that we want the individual to increase or develop, a key to any intervention strategy. By trying to do it in terms

of specific images it forces more concrete consideration of alternatives that are practicable for this particular person. Sometimes, just by asking this question, it becomes obvious what support strategies should be put in place.

There are therefore a number of tools for drawing out the 'behavioral' information held by those who know the person well. These ideally would be used in conjunction with other techniques such as participant observation and incident recording, direct environmental manipulation or independent observation and recording. However, in many service settings these other tools can be difficult to implement, so that in practice a lot of assessment relies upon the skilled use of techniques that draw from others what they know.

OBSERVATION AND RECORDING DURING STRUCTURED ENVIRONMENTAL MANIPULATION (ANALOG ASSESSMENT)

In the late 1950s/early 1960s a group of researchers around Gershon Berkson studied how short-term environmental changes such as making activities available or increasing social contact impacted upon the stereotyped movement patterns of the people with disabilities living in institutions. It was interesting work as it suggested that these behaviors were not of a single class but varied in function: some being a way of having something interesting to do (self-stimulation), some being a way of reducing stress. This work was taken further by a group of behaviorist researchers in the 1980s, led by Brian Iwata, who refined the techniques and relabeled them 'analog assessment'.

Analog assessment seeks to isolate some of the immediate influences over behavior, in particular reinforcement, by systematically varying one aspect of the environment in otherwise stable conditions and looking at the behavior frequency across a range of such variations. Assessment takes place in a series of specific sessions. Early examples compared behavior when the person was alone with nothing to do, when demands were made on her, when attention was given following the behavior in question and then some kind of control condition (for example, materials available, no demands, non-contingent attention). A function would be inferred if the behavior frequencies were elevated in one or more conditions compared with the control condition –

self-stimulation if raised in the alone condition, demand escape if raised in the demand condition, attention seeking if raised in the contingent attention condition. Since the early studies the method has been explored and refined. Although this is a potentially powerful tool for investigating the impact of immediate environmental contributors, there are a number of problems.

There are the ethical problems of deliberately setting about to provoke a behavior that is deemed not to be in the person's best interest. There are practical problems in having the personnel and expertise available to design and carry out this form of assessment. It is also only really applicable to relatively high rate behaviors that are not too dangerous (this probably constitutes a small fraction of those behaviors that practitioners are dealing with in the real world). Even for those whose behavior might be suited to this approach it has been a matter of dispute as to how often the methodology succeeds in identifying clear functions. There have also been concerns about how solid the information is – whether behavior in 'sessions' is typical of behavior in the natural environment, whether the same results hold up over time and whether the results obtained agree with the results of other forms of assessment.

Thus for many reasons analog assessment may not be part of the usual tool box in ordinary family and service settings. However, it is a useful option to know about and may have a role in teasing out immediate influences when it is not at all clear whether certain factors are contributors or not. A good example of this was a personal experience many years ago when colleagues used this type of assessment to tease out whether mild self-injury in a young girl with Rett's syndrome was triggered by social proximity or social demands. In the natural course of events, when adult staff would approach a young child with such profound difficulties, it would be to encourage engagement in some social game or play activity – proximity and demand would always go together. By planning and systematically varying how the adults approached it was possible to show that proximity was enough to raise the likelihood of the behavior – just being within a certain distance was enough. This in turn opened up strategies of support that looked at exactly how the young lady was approached and what could be done to make proximity more fun, before getting into teaching and developmental tasks.

In order to design, implement and evaluate analogs it is quite likely that a family or ordinary service setting would need some extra help. Thus far, many of the assessment tools that we have described could be used by the participants in ordinary settings, using them for themselves to find out how best to support the individual. That is not so easy with analog assessment. However, quite often, someone's behavior will trigger the entry of new people into the person's life, people charged specifically with carrying out assessment work – psychologist, psychiatrist, behavior analyst, specialists of one sort or another. They may carry out interviews with the person and those who support him. They may help with the interpretation of incident records. They will spend time observing the person. This observation may be relatively informal – a way of getting to know the person and the situation better. However, direct observation may be used more formally to collect information that will yield insight as to the contributors to the behavior in question.

Analog assessment is one such approach but there are other, more naturalistic, assessment approaches that external observers may contribute.

OBSERVATION AND RECORDING BY EXTERNAL OBSERVERS

Given that key contributors to behavior lie in the sequences of interactions and events (the focus of the present section), research workers have over the years developed a number of schemes to enable an observer to code events in sequence and to study the association between specific events and behavior. An early and outstanding scheme came from Gerald Patterson and his group who looked at the 'coercive' nature of the interactions involved in establishing and maintaining conduct difficulties in children and adolescents living with their families. The observational scheme was complex but generated solid information. However, it required a lot of training both to gather the data and to analyze it and as an assessment tool it made little impact on ordinary assessment practice.

The development of portable, powerful computers resurrected interest in the development of coherent, structured observational assessment. The computer makes the gathering of the information a little easier but it impacts massively upon the analysis of the data gathered. A number of software programs have been developed for these purposes (see Thompson, Felce and Symons 2000 for a detailed review). Although at present these tools (like Patterson's) tend to be used by highly trained specialists it seems likely that the previous barriers to accessibility will erode and that these may become tools that many more practitioners will find themselves able to use.

Computers and observation

The trade-off that users often face when considering the use of computers for collecting observational data is that between functionality and user friendliness. Some software packages allow a great deal of flexibility in terms of how data are collected – for example, different sampling methods, nested subcategories, conditional qualifiers. There may be a steep learning curve associated with using such systems. They often remain a tool for 'system experts' rather than for those who may be better placed both to know what sort of data would be worth collecting and to be able to collect it. In practice this means that important and interesting data may only be collected at the point where a behavior has become so problematic that extra specialists have been brought in to help.

There are, however, a number of software packages that are very easy to use and their development has been greatly aided by the increasing prevalence of graphical user interface operating systems. At the simplest level these involve deciding which character key on the computer keyboard to associate with a particular behavior. When the behavior occurs the key is pressed or clicked with the mouse. This would be event recording and locates the behavior in time relative to itself or to other behaviors. Duration recording can be effected by pressing the key at the start of the behavior and then pressing again when the behavior ends. Compared with traditional 'paper and pencil' recording, key pressing/clicking enables the observer to concentrate more on observation itself and to record multiple behaviors simultaneously (with practice!).

Once the data are collected, producing a summary in terms of graphical presentation or descriptive statistics is usually only a button click or two away. Most observational software packages will produce descriptive summary statistics such as percentage occurrence for the behaviors observed. Where multiple behaviors have been observed these are usually best 'eyeballed' by using simple graphs. The type of graph will depend partly upon the type of data collected (events, durations or a mixture of both) and partly upon whether one is interested in co-occurrences of behaviors. For example, Martin *et al.* (2000) offer a variety of ways to graph data and Figure 4.3 illustrates a temporal display of several behaviors in relation to one another.

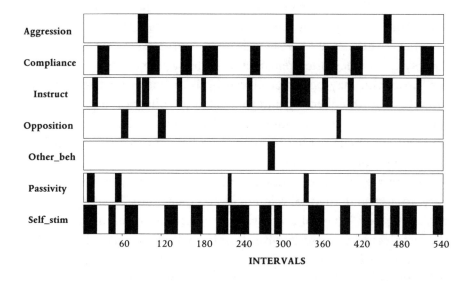

Figure 4.3: Temporal occurrence display

For many purposes, eyeballing the data may be adequate – for example, if one wants to see whether a behavior occurs differentially across settings or whether a particular intervention is resulting in more/less behavior. There may be times when more sophisticated types of analyses are helpful. There are a variety of such analyses that can be applied to continuously recorded observational data. For present purposes one particular tool will be considered – lag analysis.

Lag analysis illuminates the relationships between behaviors in terms of their relative occurrences. This is effected by determining whether the probability that one target behavior will follow another (the conditional probability) is significantly different from the overall likelihood that the target behavior will occur anyway (the unconditional probability). The conditional probabilities for the occurrence of a target behavior are calculated at different points in time relative to the first behavior (time lags) or at different points in the sequence of behaviors (event lags). It thus becomes possible to see the influence of one behavior on another at different points in time or within the sequence of recorded behaviors. An example of time lag analysis using the Martin *et al.* (2000) software package is presented in Figure 4.4. This shows the conditional probabilities of self-injurious behavior (SIB) before (lags -10 to -1), at the same time as (lag 0) and following (lags 1 to 10) attention. Each lagged interval is ten seconds and the graph shows clearly that attention reduces the probability of SIB occurring below that expected by chance (the unconditional probability).

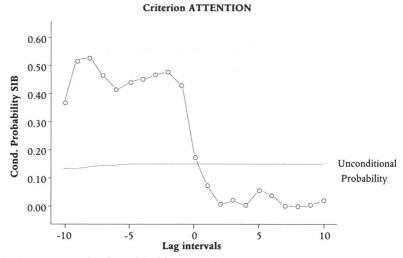

Figure 4.4: Example of graphical lag analysis

Computer assisted observation may raise the quality of assessment in many ways. It may illuminate relationships not easily accessible to the 'naked eye'. It makes it easier to see if the same relationships emerge from different observation 'sessions'. It makes it easier to assess the reliability of observational data. Some software packages will compare two observers' records of the same session and produce statistics on inter-observer agreement, an onerous task to complete by hand. Thus portable computers running observation recording and analysis software offer a new and potentially powerful tool for accurately identifying immediate and short-term factors contributing to the behavior of concern.

Thus far we have focused on tools that help us to gather information about the immediate and short-term contributors to behavioral incidents. However, our framework acknowledged that some of the contributors are longer-term factors, both features of the environment and features of the individual. Thus our assessment needs to encompass such factors and it is to this area that we now turn.

The assessment of longer-term contributors

In Chapter 3 we identified the following longer-term contributors, some sustained or recurring, others more discrete and transient. These are summarized in Table 4.3.

Table 4.3: Longer-term contributors to behavioral functioning

---

Social systems

Quality of life

Personality

Personal competences

Physical health

Mental health

Life events – major incidents and daily hassles

These potential contributors can represent a considerable challenge to the assessment process in ordinary family and service contexts. The assessment of some of these of course needs to be carried out by specialized professional practitioners (for example, physical and mental health). This would also be true if one wanted to look at social systems from the point of view of systemic family therapy. In other areas such as quality of life there are well-developed research instruments but their use does require some training and they are also time consuming in the context of them being one part of an overall assessment focused upon specific behavioral issues. Finally, many of these variables are not directly observable in the way that you can observe behaviors and their environmental correlates. The variables are more conceptual and are inferred from observations – satisfaction, systemic conflict, extroversion, depression are not themselves directly observable but are terms ascribed on the basis of rules that link observations to the defined concepts. The rules that link observations to such concepts are not always spelled out and, even if spelled out, different people may use different linkage rules (definitions).

For a practically oriented text this presents a dilemma. It would be easily resolved by taking a strict positivist behavioral perspective and sticking only to observables in the assessment process. It would be just as easy to resolve it by accepting the importance of these areas of assessment but concluding that each area should be assessed by a relevant specialist. Both of these resolutions would guarantee that most assessments of behavior for people with developmental disabilities would not include such variables.

What this text will try to do is to suggest some basic questions to ask and observations to make that will help those involved in the everyday life of the individual to identify whether there are some obvious contributors at this level. This is no substitute for specialized assessments. However, it will help to raise awareness of some of these contributors. This in turn will enhance understanding and open up approaches to support that might not be immediately obvious but that will make a significant contribution to the individual's functioning and well-being. This will become clearer in Chapter 6 which will show how manageable assessments can be done across a wide range of variables and that this can have very practical implications for the support strategies that are developed.

SOCIAL SYSTEM CHARACTERISTICS

People are often part of a number of social systems – family, workplace, school and class within school, club or society, group home. Any of the systems that are central to the person's life – in which the person spends a lot of time and is known intimately by others – will have a very significant impact on the individual's well-being and functioning. Some of the characteristics of systems that are important to consider are detailed in Table 4.4.

Table 4.4: Some important social system characteristics

Conflict level – a system that is marked by overt conflicts and disagreements that are not resolved, a 'system at war', will raise the likelihood of one or more participants acting out and/or being perceived as a problem.

Expressed emotions – some people will find it hard to cope in systems where other participants experience and express strong emotions, especially negative emotions. This kind of intense atmosphere will overwhelm some people.

Warmth and value – a system where many relationships are marked by lack of warmth, where they are predominantly clinical or devaluing, will make it hard for an individual to sustain a sense of well-being if the system is the main source of personal relationships. Systems with a strong underpinning value set that supports warm personal relationships will optimize individual functioning.

Power and control – a system where each member can influence the other, where there are clear limits and mechanisms for resolving conflicts and where power is distributed will optimize individual functioning. A system in chaos – no rules, no mechanisms for conflict resolution – will be difficult for many people to cope with. A dictatorship where all decisions are in the hands of one element in the system and that element pursues only its own satisfactions, with no curbs and with no one else's needs considered, will generate behavioral dysfunction in both the dictator and the 'subjects'. It is important to note that people with disabilities can sometimes be in the tyrant role, although more commonly they are 'subjects'.

Obviously assessing such dynamics can be difficult. However, in the present context all that is being suggested is that those carrying out the assessment observe relationships around the person and consider whether any of the dysfunctional extremes mentioned above apply in the person's situation. Figure 4.5 turns these ideas into a rating scale format.

Each question is rated on a 5-point scale:
1 Not true at all
2 True to a small extent
3 True to some extent
4 Quite true
5 Very true

Conflict level:

This system is marked by a lot of conflict and disagreements and people trying to undermine each other:

    1   2   3   4   5

Expressed emotions:

There is an intense emotional atmosphere, people express their emotions, especially their negative emotions, in a very intense way, there is a lot of criticism and upset:

    1   2   3   4   5

Warmth and value:

Relationships in this system are marked by respect and warmth, they are generally positive and enjoyed, even if there are conflicts/ disagreements about specific issues:

    1   2   3   4   5

Power and control:

This is a system in chaos with no clear/consistent limits and boundaries and no organized way of dealing with conflicts/concerns:

    1   2   3   4   5

One person in this system has complete control over what goes on and acts in any way he pleases without regard for the needs of others:

    1   2   3   4   5

Figure 4.5: Rating social system characteristics

There have been instruments to try to assess these variables in a more generalizable way (the work of Rudy Moos was seminal in this respect). However, they are not readily available now and have mainly been used in research studies – hence the present 'job aid'. It is a crude way of reminding us that behavioral issues need to be seen in the broader context of the social network and dynamics within which the individual is held. Similar considerations apply to the assessment of quality of life.

QUALITY OF LIFE

This is another huge topic and one to which researchers devote their professional lives – defining it, measuring it, exploring its determinants. As mentioned above, for present purposes our need is to identify whether present behavior is influenced by the overall quality of life that the individual leads.

There are three important elements when considering quality of life. The first is the objective 'standard of living'. We know that poverty, unemployment and social isolation are associated in humans with poor physical and mental health and socially challenging behavioral difficulties. Many people with disabilities are poor, unemployed and socially isolated. This crude association has spurred much research into the key dimensions of life quality. This work is accessibly summarized in two volumes edited by Professor Robert Schalock (Schalock 1996, 1997). The core components of life quality that hold up in many studies in a number of developed, capitalist cultures are summarized in Table 4.5 (drawn from Schalock 1996).

Assessing such factors is likely to involve observation of the individual's life and discussion with those involved in the person's life. However, such information speaks mainly to the objective standards of life. An equally significant issue is the individual's satisfaction with her life. Thus for each element of life quality mentioned above, it is important to ask – is the present situation a source of satisfaction/dissatisfaction for the person? This is particularly crucial when considering contributors to behavioral concerns, as much behavior is about the individual expressing some sense of dissatisfaction. Looking at short-term factors helps us to identify immediate dissatisfactions ('I don't like being told what to do', 'I hate having nothing to do'), but beneath these immediate dissatisfactions may lie more global dissatisfactions ('I just don't have any control in my life', 'This place is a boring dump'). Such global dissatisfactions are not necessarily consciously experienced or analyzed. Humans are rarely aware of all the things that influence their feelings and behavior. Awareness is not the issue. Assessment needs to look for the possibility that broader quality of life issues may be contributing to the 'incidents' that we observe.

Table 4.5: Quality of life dimensions

Material standards	Income, employment, possessions, housing and ownership, food, security
Social relationships	Size and diversity of network, access to family, friends, affections and intimacy
Social inclusion	Living environment, work environment, leisure environment, roles
Physical health	Nutritional status, general health, access to health care, specific health difficulties, mobility, fitness
Personal development	Personal competence, educational standard attained, access to learning opportunities, access to purposeful activity, aspirations
Emotional well-being	Happiness, safety, spirituality, stress level, self-image
Self-determination	Autonomy, choices, personal control over decisions
Rights	Privacy, voting, access, due process, ownership

There are many published assessment formats for quality of life. In practice much of this information may already be available in notes, charts and other individual assessment formats (individual program plans, person centered plans). If not, it is certainly an area about which to gather information and the text above details the areas about which information will be needed.

There is a third element to quality of life that is much harder to define and assess. That is the concept of niche or person–environment fit. It is captured to some extent in the assessment of satisfaction with quality of life but not entirely. It is a more global notion. Human beings function well if they find the niche that works for them – the kinds of relationships, environments, activities and pace of life that deliver the 'feelgood' factor. A person with autism who is also an urban raised, sensation seeking extrovert with a short attention span and a lust for the outrageous is simply not going to function well in a village community that emphasizes peace and harmony, New Age music and weaving, even if it does call itself a special place for people with autism. Thus when we have looked at the objective and subjective aspects of quality of life we still need to ask:

> *Is this the kind of life that really suits the person about whom we are concerned? What things make sense and what things make no sense in this person's current life? What would be the ideal life for this person or a life that would generally work well?*

If there is a big gap between life now and the life that would work, if there are a number of things going on that make no sense for this person, this indicates potentially important contributors to the behaviors that we are identifying as problematic. It will also serve as a sharp reminder that the life that would work for the person may be very different from the lives that work for his parents and those who support him. Not everyone aspires to fulfilling their potential, working hard, owning a house and having deep meaningful relationships. There are plenty of loafers, lounge lizards, charlatans and lotus-eaters in this world. Indeed it is just such diversity that makes life interesting. There is no reason to believe that people with disabilities have to be regarded as automatically sharing the dreams of the Caucasian chattering classes.

PERSONALITY

The concept of niche led us to invoke personal characteristics (sensation seeking extrovert) that are usually described under the heading of 'personality'. These are considered more enduring characteristics of the person that are linked to core motivations – extroverts are motivated to make a lot of social contacts and seek a lot of social involvement; introverts may seek more solitary activities and social engagement with a small circle of like-minded folk. This is not to say that extroverts cannot function when alone and that introverts never go to parties, but in general, social contact is more motivating for one as opposed to the other.

This is a very big area in general psychology and there is much dispute as to what constitutes the main dimensions of personality. Eysenck has suggested three core dimensions:

- Extroversion/introversion – the degree to which the person seeks social engagement/stimulation.

- Neuroticism – the amount of anxiety that is evoked in the course of everyday life.

- Psychoticism – the degree of social sensitivity/empathy.

Many others have suggested a 'big five':

- Extroversion –- as above.

- Agreeableness – how pleasant and cooperative someone generally is.

- Conscientiousness – how thorough, diligent and achievement oriented the person is.

- Emotional stability – how easily upset the person is.

- Sophistication – how drawn the person is to intellectual and artistic interests.

Finally, Mehrabian has suggested a three-factor approach, one that the present author finds helpful:

- Pleasure–displeasure – the predisposition to experience positive or negative emotions.

- Arousability – the intensity of emotions experienced, the reactivity of the person.

- Dominance–submissiveness – the degree to which one has expectations of control and influence over events and outcomes.

All these views of personality have generated measurement devices. By and large these devices are self-report questionnaires or rating scales which are hard to access for most people with developmental disabilities. Figure 4.6 offers a job aid that draws on the concepts prevalent in mainstream psychology described above and would be completed by someone who knows the person well. Whilst not exactly a sophisticated measurement tool, it at least acts as a reminder of the importance of this area. To illustrate the point, if assessment of short-term factors suggests that a behavior is maintained by the social response that it achieves, the plan of support might be influenced by our understanding of the individual's personality type. If the person was recognized as an extrovert then we will need to accept that high levels of social input are needed and our plan has to be to shape acceptable ways of eliciting social response. If, however, the person is not an extrovert but high on dominance then what they may be seeking is not 'attention' but 'control' and our plan will need to address how the person can take more control in his life.

Each item is rated along a line with the end points defined – the left end X represents **not true at all**, the right end X represents **definitely true**.

This individual:

Loves social contact and engagement, prefers to hang out with others rather than be alone:

X   X

Is generally amenable and cooperative with other people:

X   X

Is easily stressed or upset, worries a lot, has a lot of fears or anxieties:

X   X

Tends to experience many negative emotions and rarely seems to experience pleasure or enjoyment:

X   X

Is very driven by the need to control other people and what goes on in life:

X   X

Is very sensitive to the needs of others, is careful not to hurt animals:

X   X

Experiences strong emotions, is emotionally volatile or intense (includes both enjoyments and upsets):

X   X

Prefers strong stimulation and lots of excitement:

X   X

Tends to be task focused, wants to learn and likes to complete tasks and complete them correctly:

X   X

Figure 4.6: Personality rating scale

As well as these more general characteristics, the assessment information should also identify the specific things that the person currently seeks out or seeks to avoid (reinforcer preferences). Such information is often available already in many services. However, its quality is extremely variable and therefore it is important to check it for:

- Completeness – are there other things that the person currently has strong preferences for?

- Validity – is there evidence that the person actually seeks or seeks to escape/avoid the items identified as likes and dislikes?

Beliefs about preferences should always be cross-checked against the person's observed behavior.

PERSONAL COMPETENCES

In judging the dilemmas that the person faces and that are being expressed behaviorally it will be important to have an overview of what the person can and cannot do and how that maps onto their everyday personal priorities – their preferences and concerns. To what extent does the person have the tools to deal with these issues in a way that others will find acceptable?

There are a large number of such assessment devices designed specifically in the field of developmental disabilities and most service settings these days will include in their routine work a detailed assessment of personal competence.

From a behavioral perspective there are some key areas that directly impact upon behavioral functioning. Whilst these are covered to some extent in 'the usual checklists' they are not always included, or not included in a way that makes clear their relevance to the sorts of behaviors that give rise to concern in others. The areas in question are the following.

1. Communication

It is important to know the skills a person has to get his messages over. It is equally important to know in some detail what exactly the person does and does not understand of the verbal input that others direct to him. Many problems arise when communication breaks down, either when the individual cannot get his message across in a way that others understand, or when he fails to understand or misunderstands the messages that others try to convey to him. Thus comprehension is as important as expression. It is also important to know what it is that the person most often initiates communication about, however he does it (words, signs, gestures, behaviors) – what are the main topics from the individual's point of view, what is central to that person's agenda? So often we enter the lives of people with disabilities full of our own agenda, knowing what is best for them and what is important in life. The other person may have a very different agenda, no less valid than our own and central to our understanding of how he experiences the world.

> *My agenda may be about teaching you skills so that you can be independent. Your agenda may be about what food you are having and when you are having it. If I am not aware of the big issues for you then we are likely to end up in conflict, which you may deal with by a behavior that I will call problematic.*

Communication skills assessments often fail to identify the key subjects for the person.

2. Emotional management

Many behavioral problems arise in the context of heightened emotional arousal and may be described as a 'loss of control'. It is all too easy to assume that the person lacks self-control, yet close observation will indicate that many people – even those who may be regarded as profoundly impacted by their disabilities, with no speech and very limited understanding of what others say to them – show some skills at both recognizing increased arousal and taking steps to avoid loss of control. The most common tactics are withdrawing from the situation (leaving the room), increasing repetitive hand and body movements (sometimes dismissed as 'stereotypies') or restraining a limb or the whole body that may be implicated in loss of control (sitting on hands, positioning self in a corner behind a desk). Teaching people new self-control skills is a long process. It is easier if we can build on the skills that they already have, recognize them when they occur and facilitate their use of the skills. It is therefore important that assessments of competence include assessment of the skills the person already shows for both the recognition of escalating arousal and the ability to deal with it in a constructive way.

3. Self-occupation

Likewise the abilities that the individual has to occupy himself independently, without support, for more than a few minutes. Many behaviors arise in unstructured situations when the individual does not have much to do and the support available is limited. Of course we may want to structure time better and increase the availability of support but in any real world there will be 'down time'. It is therefore important to assess what things the person can do without support and for how long – a key intervention may be to make sure that these things are available, perhaps only available, at down times.

> *One of the most ludicrous experiences you can have is to watch autistic children in school go through a lesson called 'prevocational skills', where they are encouraged to match, sort and assemble (not pre any vocation this author has ever come across... but that's another story), skills they acquire anyway without support and activities in which they will often engage even if no one is around. Then all these great self-occupation materials are put away and the children go to 'recess' when there is nothing that they can engage with, not many people around to support; and of course where all hell breaks loose on a regular basis!*

Thus careful assessment of self-occupation competence is an important assessment element in behaviorally focused work.

4. Social understanding

We all come close to losing control several or more times a week. What stops us? In part the emotional management skills that we described in '2. Emotional Management' but also our understanding of how others will feel if we act out, what they will think of us, what we will think of ourselves and what social consequences may befall us further down the line (rejection, arrest, jail). Social awareness and understanding are a key inhibitory resource. Without that resource we are much more likely to act as we feel at the moment. Equipping people with that resource becomes therefore an important focus in behavioral work. Unfortunately it has received very little attention from an assessment point of view, other than in diagnosing such phenomena as autism or personality disorders. These kinds of diagnostic assessments do not really help in identifying competences to build on.

The aspects of personal competence emphasized above are absent from many 'off the shelf' skills assessments. We have made a small attempt to remedy this in the Behavioral Explorer, detailed further in Chapter 6. We would also encourage readers to add these elements to the skills assessment that they are already using so that the information becomes more routinely available when behavior becomes a focus.

PHYSICAL AND MENTAL HEALTH

Any assessment of significant and enduring behavioral difficulties must include assessment of health issues. These require the input of qualified professionals and no do-it-yourself diagnosis kit will be offered here! However, the Behavioral Explorer (Chapter 6) provides a section for entering identified physical health difficulties, to make sure that they feature in the analysis of the behavior. It also includes a section on the emotional experience of the individual. Whilst people with developmental disabilities may have diagnosable mental health problems it is important not to pathologize all emotional experiences, even extreme ones – extreme anger, extreme sadness, extreme elation are not necessarily abnormal. Gaining insight into the emotional world of the person is an important goal of assessment, aside from whether this may be categorized as a psychiatric disorder. The Behavioral Explorer seeks to draw out information about the emotions that we see portrayed in everyday life – the type(s) of emotion, the things that elicit these emotions, the frequency and intensity of their presentation. This again empowers our insight into the person's agenda – the things that are important to her. It also gives us a sense of the balance of emotional experience. Sometimes when you do this assessment it reveals that almost all the emotions that you see are negative and you realize that life for the person is full of distress. This may reflect their personality type or the way life is (hence is seen in the context of the assessment of personality and quality of life). Whether or not it justifies a mental health categorization is a separate question. A serious emotional imbalance that links to the behaviors of concern can be an area of intervention in everyday life, not necessarily involving the pharmaceutical industry (see Clements and Zarkowska 2000).

LIFE EVENTS

The final area that we included under the longer-term, more distal influences is life events. There are life event assessments that some may want to use. Usually practitioners will have some of this information available and it is simply a matter of drawing it into our perspectives on the current behavior(s) of concern. There are three important types of event that will impact emotional well-being and behavioral functioning:

1. Trauma/abuse – the experience of trauma and abuse can impact upon behavioral and emotional functioning over many years. It is therefore important to know if the person has ever been exposed to such events.

2. Recent upheavals – significant changes and losses can impact upon behavioral functioning over an extended period of time (two to three years as a crude guideline). It is therefore important to document all such events known to have occurred in the last two to three years.

3. Daily hassles – it is not just the big things that undermine coping resources but the accumulation of irritants occurring on a day-to-day basis. This is more difficult to assess satisfactorily but it is worth considering the extent to which life at present runs fairly smoothly or is filled with conflicts and things not going right (aside from what goes on around incidents of the behaviors of concern – this is a broader view of how life is at present).

Establishing the significance of longer-term influences

When looking at the shorter-term influences over behavior there are ways of establishing the likelihood of some sort of causal association between events and behavior. It can be difficult but at least there is some possibility of demonstrating the likelihood of a link. These methods are a lot stronger for the computer based assessment tools that build in powerful analytic methods.

However, when it comes to the longer-term factors it is much more difficult to be certain about causal contributions. The assessment can establish whether certain factors are present, for example:

- conflicted social system
- poor quality of life
- volatile, control oriented personality type
- poor communication skills
- limited social understanding
- dominance of negative emotions
- many upheavals in the last two years.

Whether these are in any way relevant to the behavior in question will be a matter of judgment. The basis for the judgment will not be statistical. It will be based upon psychological plausibility – whether we can see links between the longer-term factors and the shorter-term influences involved in the drama we call 'incidents'; whether putting these things together makes some kind of psychological sense.

We will take a further look at this in Chapter 5. However, it is important not to be too overwhelmed by the subjective nature of the interpretation of longer-term influences. There are relatively accessible 'common sense' standards – it is not a matter of deep, complex psychological understanding. The status of the judgment also needs to be re-emphasized. When we identify a contributing factor we are not making a statement about truth. We are hypothesizing. We are saying that it is our hypothesis that there is an association. If we follow through on this hypothesis, if we act as though it were true – if we resolve the conflicts in the social system – and the behavior changes, then at least we were not completely on the wrong track. If we resolve the conflicts and nothing changes, then it is harder to continue to believe that social conflicts are contributing to the behavior in question (though they may be contributing to other problems). In this way the person about whom we are hypothesizing speaks to us directly through her behavior. She informs us whether our plausible hypothesis is still as plausible as it was before. Her observable behavior is the bottom line against which our theories are judged. That is why, in behavioral work, it is important not to be overattached to our interpretations, to be ready to look at things another way and always to listen carefully to what the person is telling us by words or deeds.

Concluding remarks

To do a competent job of assessing behavior we need to know what kinds of information to gather and we need tools that will help us gather this information accurately. Over time individual practitioners will develop their own tool kit, the methods and formats that they can understand and that they find useful in solving the puzzle called 'behavior'. We have sought in this chapter to describe some of the available tools and to provide some additional tools. More materials can be found in Chapter 6, in the Appendices and in some of the items referenced in the Resources list. There is no pretence at being exhaustive. Rather it is hoped that there is enough information to enable an ordinary practitioner to get to work on identifying many of the likely contributors to a behavior of concern. This requires assembling a large amount of potentially relevant information. However, before this can become useful to the person whose behavior is of concern, before rational support plans can be identified and implemented, this mass of information has to be summarized. From all that has been discovered, the most likely contributors have to be extracted and it is this step that the next chapter examines.

CHAPTER 5

Extracting Meaning from the Information Gathered

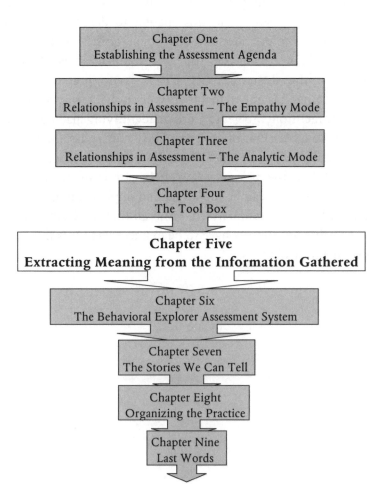

The assessment work detailed in this book will generate a large volume of information about the individual whose behavior is cause for concern and about her life and circumstances. This information will be of general value in helping us to understand this person better. However, the purpose of a behavioral assessment is to construct an explanation for the occurrence of one or more specific behaviors. It may be generally useful to know that the individual is an extrovert who loves social engagement and has a short attention span, but is that in any way relevant to understanding why the person on occasion bites other people? Gathering wide-ranging, quality information is a first step. That information then needs to be reviewed and analyzed so that the likely contributors to the behavior(s) of concern can be extracted.

Introductory remarks

Although many services gather information about behavior it is less common for the meaning of that information to be carefully analyzed and summarized, especially if the service does not have a 'designated behaviorhitter' (psychologist, behavior analyst, psychiatrist, behavior consultant). An important first step is therefore to clarify whose job it is to extract meaning from the information gathered. It could be the job of an individual or of a small group. It is unlikely that a large group could effectively carry out such an operation. If it is not clear whose job it is, then it is unlikely that it will turn out to be anyone's job. Decisions about interventions will then be based upon the judgments/intuitions/gut feelings of individuals or factions in the support system. This negates the whole purpose of systematic assessment and reduces the likelihood that the decisions made will be competent. People with disabilities whose behavior causes serious concern cannot afford that degree of incompetence from the people paid to support them. The work of analyzing and summarizing information must be allocated and no decisions on the actions to take should be made until that work is completed.

It is important also to understand the kind of explanation that we are looking for. This book is based around the notion of 'messy' explanations – that behavior is an outcome that results from the operation of several factors that might interact, accumulate or work in parallel. The exercise in Chapter 3 tried to illustrate this point. The answer to 'Why does X do that?' will contain several elements – a rough guide is that the answer will usually contain somewhere between five and nine elements, less often three to eleven (with acknowledgements to George Miller's classic paper, *The Magical Number Seven, Plus or Minus Two*). There is no assumption that these elements are arranged in a hierarchy – that some are 'surface' and others 'underlying' – although in our summary we should try to look at whether and how the factors link together. There is therefore no assumption of a single, underlying cause that is the main target of intervention. Rather the contributory factors identified will indicate a range of issues to address, a number of supports to provide.

We need to be clear about the status of the summary of contributory factors that we derive and how we judge its value. Certainly the contributory factors should meet an initial standard of 'psychological plausibility'. They should tell a story that makes some kind of 'person sense'. Following the example above, if we think that it is relevant to the behavior that the person is an extrovert who loves social engagement and has a short attention span, then there would be a strain on the story if we felt that the biting was maintained by escape from social situations. This is not an impossible combination but it is also not a natural fit. Therefore, as we look at our assembled contributory factors we should be able to recognize some kind of ordinary human story, something that says, 'Yes, this is how people are.'

> *People who have had dramatic upheavals in their lives and are now around people who do not like them and are doing things that they do not like may well feel miserable and angry and vent their frustrations on others.*

> *People who love exciting visual stimulation and who do not read other people's feelings terribly well may well do things to others that produce great sensory effects but are a disaster socially.*

However, a plausible story is not necessarily 'right'. At the end of the day the individual tells us through his behavior whether we are on the right track. The status of our story is that it is one possible story; it is a hypothesis, a working theory. It needs to be tested against reality. If this story is true, what should we do if we want to help the individual move on from behaving in that way, if we want the behavior of concern to occur less often and/or less intensely? We need to spell out the practical implications of the story that we are telling. We then follow through on these practical implications – we do the things that the story would indicate to be relevant. If the behavior changes, then there is some indication that we are on the right track. If we follow through and the behavior does not change, then maybe we just need to persist a little longer or try something else that seems relevant; or maybe we got the story wrong and we need to look again, do some more assessment, look for another story. This is how the individual 'speaks' to us through behavior. The work is like the childhood game where we are guided to success by 'warmer'/'colder' feedback. Monitoring behavior thus becomes an exercise in listening and guidance. It is more a human dialog than a scientific analysis.

It is therefore important not to be overly attached to a story or explanation. It may be right; it may be wrong. We may have to change our minds. This spirit of inquiry, this flexibility needs to be taken on board by all those who would seek to be helpful to those who trouble us by their behavior. Too often egos get involved and there is a competition as to who is 'right'. Such ego battles, which are about the needs of supporters, do nothing but harm to the people whose needs the supporters are charged with identifying and meeting. It is not about who is right. It is about getting it right for the individual.

Building the story

This section will look at one way of building the story. It is not the only way and readers may have a better way of doing this. However, if you have no experience of sifting through a large quantity of information and extracting the elements that are significant for the behavior of concern, then this section may help to get you started. Our approach will be to work systematically through the time frames described in Chapter 3:

- immediate influences
- short-term influences
- longer-term influences.

Immediate influences

The first step is looking at the incident records and any questionnaire or interview information that we have gathered about the immediate circumstances surrounding incidents – the antecedents and consequences, triggers and results, discriminative stimuli/establishing operations and reinforcements. The assessment protocol presented in Appendix 2 helps to guide the extraction of specific contributors and Appendix 1 offers a guide for summarizing the data from incident record forms. It is important to remember when analyzing incidents that we are looking for 'strong themes'. Not every incident will fit the theme – there are often 'outliers' that are not easily explained. It is important at this stage not to insist on explanations that cover 100 percent of incidents, as we need to get to work on the strong themes, picking up the less obvious issues later. If we insist on the 100 percent criterion then assessment tends to go on forever and the momentum of support can be lost.

The first question is whether the behavior looks like it is maintained by some sort of reinforcing event or whether it looks more like overarousal and loss of control, without an obvious reinforcement component (see Chapter 3). This is a difficult judgment and will require attention to both what happens just before and what happens just after incidents (rather than looking at 'consequences' in isolation).

If it looks as if there are reinforcing consequences, then it is important to specify what those are. Table 5.1 illustrates a crude categorization of reinforcers with some examples. Reinforcers may be social or physical and the change may be an addition (positive reinforcement) or a removal (negative reinforcement). However, within those categories there are many different specific transactions that reflect the great variety of individual differences between people. At this stage of the analysis it is important to spell out as specifically as possible the social or physical changes that the behavior creates and that we believe to reinforce that behavior. There may be more than one type of reinforcement for the behavior – some behaviors are multifunctional, all-purpose tools for getting things to change in the way that the individual prefers.

Table 5.1: Examples of reinforcing events and processes		
	ADD	**REMOVE**
SOCIAL	Reassurance Praise Gratitude Focal attention Help in problem solving	Demands Intrusions Conversation Correction Limit setting
PHYSICAL	Preferred Noise Visual stimulation Movement stimulation Tactile stimulation Activity Food/drink	Disliked Noise Visual stimulation Movement stimulation Tactile stimulation Activity Food/drink

Once reinforcers are identified, it is worth cross checking this analysis with the information that we have gathered on the reinforcer preferences and personality characteristics of the individual – for example, the things that the individual is generally known to work to get or work to get out of, the more sustained motivations that we flag up under 'personality'. When we make this comparison, we are looking for some kind of 'fit'. Are the reinforcing consequences for the specific behavior the sorts of consequences that are generally important to this person? If there is not a 'fit' it does not mean that our analysis of the incidents is wrong (after all, even happy-go-lucky extroverts get depressed sometimes!) but it would suggest that we should recheck the incident analysis, to be quite sure.

Once the reinforcing consequences have been identified, the specific antecedents that predict the likelihood of incidents should also be noted. Incident records will often pick up specific events that lead to incidents. However, some key antecedents are the absence of something happening – a lack of social input for several minutes, an absence of something interesting to do for longer than five minutes. These 'absence' triggers will rarely be picked up on charts, particularly the simpler A-B-C format charts. If a clear consequence has been identified but no clear antecedent, then it will be worth interviewing those who manage the incidents to get more detail about the ongoing situation at the time.

Such antecedents or triggers perform two functions. One type of antecedent gives information to the person that an important source of reinforcement is now available if the 'right' behavior is emitted. This type of antecedent is sometimes referred to as a discriminative stimulus. Thus if an individual likes to:

- *chat*
- *smoke*
- *eat candy*
- *see things shatter*

then

- *seeing the person who will always talk to you*
- *seeing the person who smokes*
- *seeing the candies being put in the cupboard*
- *seeing the glass amidst the plastic cups*

will indicate that reinforcement is more likely to be available compared with

- *seeing the person who always ignores you*
- *seeing the person who never smokes*

- *seeing tins being put in the cupboard*

- *seeing only plastic cups.*

Other antecedents, sometimes called establishing operations, more directly prioritize a motivation; they generate the need to act.

> *It is only once someone else starts to scream that it becomes important to get out of the situation; it is only once someone is close by, talking at you and putting tasks in front of you, that it becomes important to bring intrusion to an end; it is only when no one has noticed you for five or more minutes that the need for reassurance grows strong.*

It may be helpful to understand this difference when looking to identify the immediately preceding events that seem to predict or precipitate incidents of the behaviors that are cause for concern. Both types of antecedent are important because they predict incidents occurring, even if the linkage mechanism is different.

Not all behaviors conform to this type of operant formulation. Some are better represented as escalation of arousal leading to the collapse of inhibition and loss of control. If the behavior of concern looks more like this, then the analysis of incidents needs to focus upon the antecedent side and we should extract both the environmental factors that contribute to escalating arousal and the signs that the individual gives that arousal is increasing (not always obvious and sometimes unique to individuals). Again, this information may not be readily available from some types of incident records and, in this case, interviewing those involved will be needed to pinpoint the specific factors that lead up to incidents.

From the analysis so far of the information about incidents and the immediate circumstances we will summarize the specific contributors under the headings detailed in Figure 5.1.

Once we have summary statements at this stage of analysis we move on to the next time frame.

Behavior(s) of concern:

The reinforcing consequences that we believe are maintaining the behavior:

The specific events that predict incidents occurring (immediate antecedents):

The specific events that contribute to escalating arousal:

The signs that the individual gives of escalating arousal:

Figure 5.1: Summarizing behavior assessment information

Short-term influences

Immediate influences are those that surround the incident in terms of seconds, perhaps up to a minute or two. Short-term influences move the time frame to minutes and hours (occasionally days – for example, the impact of constipation). We categorized these influences as:

EXTERNAL ENVIRONMENTAL FACTORS

- Physical – for example, noise levels, lighting conditions, temperature, aroma, space available.

- Activational – the activities available to engage with (or not).

- Organizational – the extent to which a situation is organized so that everybody knows what the situation is about and what they are to do in that situation, whether the situation has some specific purpose or not (we sometimes use the notion of structure – is the situation structured or unstructured?).

- Social – who is around and what is their availability (for example, staff handover times, activity transitions involving tidying and setting up)?

- Temporal – a transition when one activity is ending and another is about to begin; time of day, perhaps linking to individual biorhythms (early morning, after lunch, late afternoon).

INTERNAL ENVIRONMENTAL FACTORS

- Individual biorhythms and energy level – people vary in when they are most alert and energetic in a day and incidents may cluster around the highs or lows of individual biorhythms.

- Emotional states – transient moods involving tension, anxiety, anger, excitement, sadness.

- Physical states – ongoing discomforts such as blocked sinus, headache, full bowel.

When we are trying to summarize assessment information at this level, we are looking for evidence of short-term influences that strengthen the motivations identified in the analysis of immediate influences. They will act as establishing operations for reinforcement processes or contribute to the increasing arousal level that may lead to loss of control. Such influences 'set the scene' for incidents to occur (they are sometimes also called 'setting conditions'). Incidents may occur if such influences go on for too long; they can have a cumulative effect. In some cases they merge into being triggers; in other cases, there is a need for additional triggering, along the lines of 'the straw that breaks the camel's back'.

> *I have not moved my bowels for several days, it is the morning which is not my best time, we drove past a McDonald's without stopping and now you are taking me into that place where they mess about with my head and hair, which I just hate...time to act!*

The information may be available from incident records (depending upon how they are designed). It will emerge from the 'three questions' exercise and it can be extracted from interviews with those who have extensive experience of the individual and who are regularly involved in dealing with the incidents.

It must be stressed that it is not obligatory to find contributors in every category. It is also important, as mentioned earlier, that the levels of analysis link together – that there should be a plausible connection between immediate and short-term factors. Indeed this framework for extracting summary information from a wide-ranging assessment tries to ensure that such connections are made. Our summary therefore expands (see Figure 5.2).

Behavior(s) of concern:

The reinforcing consequences that we believe are maintaining the behavior:

The specific events that predict incidents occurring (immediate antecedents):

The specific events that contribute to escalating arousal:

The signs that the individual gives of escalating arousal:

Specific external environmental influences that 'set the scene' for incidents being likely to occur:

Specific internal environmental influences that 'set the scene' for incidents being likely to occur:

Figure 5.2: Expanded summary of behavior assessment information

Once we have incorporated the summary of any short-term influence we move to the final step.

Longer-term influences

We have categorized longer-term influences as:

- Social system characteristics
- Quality of life
- Personality
- Current competences

- Physical health issues
- Mental health issues
- Life events.

Because the assessment of these factors presents a considerable challenge and many of the potential approaches to such assessment are not accessible to those involved in the day-to-day lives of people with developmental disabilities, Chapters 4 and 6 devote considerable attention to 'job aids' to help look at longer-term influences. Most services will keep incident records of behaviors but there is less of a standard as to how information will be gathered on these longer-term factors. Services will vary and those charged with producing a summary of relevant contributors may have to scan a range of records and reports to get access to this kind of information (if it is available at all).

The time frame for longer term is those factors that are operating over weeks, months and in some cases years to make it more likely that the behaviors of concern occur. If those factors were not present, then the behaviors would be less likely to occur. These longer-term influences contribute to the sorts of motivations expressed through the behavior (for example, personality factors, extended states such as depression), to extended, heightened arousal (sharing your life with people that you cannot stand or get on with at all, being in a social system marked by frequent interactions involving high expressed emotions, extended states such as general anxiety disorder or an anxious personality), and to the regular recurrence of the scenarios that we have identified in the short-term and immediate analysis. This last named area requires a little more explanation.

A service that is supporting people with autism but has little understanding of what this means and is relatively unstructured and chaotic will regularly create situations in which individuals identified as autistic become stressed and disorganized and act accordingly (a social system/quality of life issue). A service whose mission focuses exclusively on a narrow area (assessment and treatment) may well generate such a poor quality of life that individuals are regularly bored, stressed or ignored, and act accordingly. A social system marked by chronic conflict and high expressed emotion will regularly generate uncomfortable emotional atmospheres and inconsistencies in responding, and that again will contribute to 'incidents'. A person who has experienced abuse and is suffering from post traumatic stress may well experience intermittent but sudden escalations in arousal, sometimes triggered by environmental cues ('flashbacks'), which in turn will lead to incidents (a life events and mental health issue). A person with chronic bowel or sinus problems will regularly lack physical well-being and this in turn will set the scene for incidents (a physical health issue). The person who lacks the skill to charm others will regularly find himself ignored or rejected; the person who lacks the skill to get over to other people important issues with which she needs help will regularly find herself uncomfortable and frustrated; the person who lacks skills in emotional management will regularly find himself overwhelmed by escalating arousal (current competence issues). These more systemic factors, whether part of the individual's own system of functioning or a characteristic of the external environment, often play a key role that will be missed if the analysis of behavior focuses only on immediate and short-term contributors.

We began the analysis with immediate and short-term factors, as there is usually better quality, more accessible information about these in most services. It is also more likely that we can compare how the person functions when these factors are present and when they are absent. We can thus feel more secure about there being some kind of causal contribution at these levels, as the factors tend to fluctuate over time; they are not constants. However, it is much more difficult to get quality information at the longer-term level and in many cases (apart from fluctuating physical and mental health issues) it is more difficult to compare the person with or without the operation of longer-term factors such as life events, personal competences, social system characteristics (sometimes a detailed history can do this). Thus, at the longer-term level, we are much more reliant on the plausibility standard for identifying potential contributors.

Our summary format can now be completed (see Figure 5.3).

Behavior(s) of concern:

The reinforcing consequences that we believe are maintaining the behavior:

The specific events that predict incidents occurring (immediate antecedents):

The specific events that contribute to escalating arousal:

The signs that the individual gives of escalating arousal:

Specific external environmental influences that 'set the scene' for incidents being likely to occur:

Specific internal environmental influences that 'set the scene' for incidents being likely to occur:

Specific longer-term factors that are definitely present and show some plausible link to the factors identified in the short-term and immediate categories:

Figure 5.3: Final summary of behavior assessment information

As we look down the summary list some plausible human story should be apparent. However, the key thing to remember is that this is a 'working theory' rather than a statement of truth. It will help to organize our support efforts in a coherent and respectful way but it is the result of those efforts that counts – whether the supports that we provide impact the behaviors of concern. This will tell us whether our theory comes close to the other's reality. If not, we may need to take another look.

From the 'story' to real world supports

The process moves on by writing next to each identified contributor the kinds of inputs that would address the issues identified.

If we believe that the behavior is maintained by sensorily exciting reinforcing consequences, we might address this by making such stimulation more freely available, teaching a more socially acceptable way of getting that experience or teaching a communication skill so that the person can ask for access to such favored activities.

If we believe that transition times are key flashpoints, we can look at how we communicate about transitions, how we prepare for transitions and whether we can develop rituals that diffuse the emotional build up around transitions.

If we believe that staff interaction style contributes, we may look to train staff, fire staff and hire more suitable people or seek to move the person into a more constructive system of support.

If we believe that life events such as loss and upheaval are contributing then we may look at how we reassure the individual, help to develop a personal history for that person ('life story' book) or help them access supportive counseling.

If we believe that unusual beliefs (for example, beliefs about persecution that have led to the person being labeled 'paranoid') contribute then we could look at how we might challenge those beliefs.

At this stage the exercise is one of brainstorming – we are generating a lot of plausible interventions based upon our 'working theory': if this were true it would lead us to... This exercise might usefully be carried out by all those involved in supporting the person. This is by way of contrast to producing the summary, which is probably better done by an individual or small group. Table 5.2 illustrates the outcome of this exercise for Gus, an individual who bites other people.

Table 5.2: Linking identified contributors to support ideas for Gus

	Specific contributor	Support ideas
Reinforcement	Escape from uncomfortable situation	Keep in the situation Remove early in the chain of arousal Teach an 'I want out' communication skill
Antecedent	Novel environments marked by a lot of noise, lights and crowds	Avoid these environments altogether Increase exposure in gradual way to build tolerance
Arousal increasers	As for antecedents	
Signs of increasing arousal	Generally increased movement, high pitched vocalization, hitting at own abdomen	Respond to these signs by removing Gus to low stimulus area Prompt use of 'I want out' communication
Short-term environmental	As for antecedents plus more likely in late afternoon	Practice exposure in mornings and daytimes at weekends
Short-term internal	Already stressed mood, bowels not having moved for 3 days or more	Take for a brisk walk before exposing to these environments Use comfort foods during exposure Increase dietary fiber Seek GI consultation

Longer term	More extended stressed mood (recurring)	Seek psychiatric consultation
	Lack of communication and emotional management skills	Teach communication skill (as above)
	Lack of general cooperativeness	Teach self-massage to calm
	Family stress level	Increase number of requests for cooperation and reinforcement for success
		Provide family counseling
		Provide practical support services to family – respite, leisure access, housework

Having generated a range of potential and plausible interventions, it is then a matter of deciding which ones will actually be implemented. The list should now be ordered in terms of priority. Priorities are allocated on the basis of which interventions we believe would have the greatest impact and which we have the resources to be getting on with right away. The resources may be physical (do we have the number of staff or the type of equipment that would enable us to do this?) or competence based (do we have the know-how to provide supportive counseling or challenge unusual beliefs?). At the top of the list will be the interventions that we believe will make an impact and that we can get on with right away. Further down will be those for which we will need extra resources or time (for example, to train staff, to effect a change of placement, to access a competent, relevant professional).

Once we have the prioritized list, those people supporting the individual then need to make a clear statement about the interventions that they will commit to implement. The final step is then to spell out who needs to do what in order to ensure that the interventions committed to are implemented in practice. Table 5.3 illustrates this for Gus.

Table 5.3: From analysis to implemented supports for Gus

Prioritized Intervention List

1. Relieve family stress

2. Teach an 'I want out' communication

3. Increase exposure

4. Increase general cooperativeness

And so on, for the other interventions regarded as plausible...

Action Planner:

Target	Who will work on and how	To be achieved by
Relieve family stress	Social worker with parents will recruit in-home support staff to work with Gus and identify a respite provision	July 12th
Teach an 'I want out' communication	Behavior consultant, language specialist and parents will identify communication mode, assemble materials and start to practice in disliked situations that are not highly stressful	June 22nd
Increase exposure	Behavior consultant, parents and in-home support staff will work out a plan to increase exposure to known high stress situations and will begin to implement	August 8th
Increase general cooperativeness	Behavior consultant and parents will identify specific domestic tasks that Gus will be asked regularly to do and will identify specific prompting and reinforcement strategies	June 1st

And then...

We have gone through the assessment information and extracted those factors that we believe to be contributing to the events that we have defined as behaviors of concern. We have spelled out what should be done if our analysis is 'true'. Finally we have committed to actually carrying out one or more of the interventions identified as plausible.

It is now a question of listening – of making sure that we implement what we have committed to and that we monitor the behaviors of concern to see if there is any discernible impact upon them. If there is, we should celebrate. If not we may need to persevere and/or add some other interventions from our list. All interventions take some time to have an effect so that immediate results are not the norm. However, if there is no sign of change after six to eight weeks that would certainly suggest adding some interventions from the original list. This would take priority over going back to the assessment. Revisiting the assessment process should only be considered if new information comes to light (perhaps as a result of the interventions carried out) that indicates clearly that our views need amending, or if many interventions have been tried over several months with absolutely no evidence of any impact at all.

The cycle – reprise

We have therefore now completed the cycle described in Chapter 1 (see Figure 5.4).

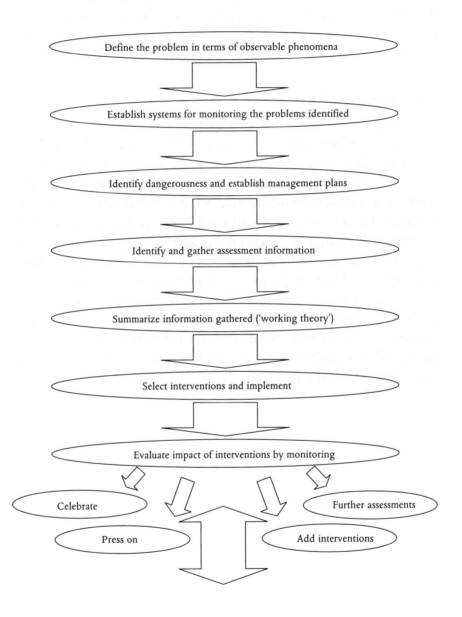

Figure 5.4 Effecting change – the activity sequence

We have moved from defining a problem to building an understanding of that problem through an assessment process and then following through on that understanding with practical interventions. From that point on we are guided by the behavioral sonar as we listen to what the person tells us about the usefulness of the supports we are offering.

Concluding remarks

In the previous chapter we offered a number of job aids for gathering assessment information that, along with commercially available materials, will help readers develop their tool boxes for this work. In the present chapter we have offered a guide for integrating and summarizing assessment information, whilst acknowledging again that this job can be done in a number of ways. The next chapter will describe an attempt to design an assessment program that guides those who support an individual through the whole process or cycle – from defining a problem through gathering information in a systematic way to summarizing and then identifying relevant action plans. This is included for illustrative purposes, to encourage others to consider designing a system that would work for them. However, it is also a program that is available commercially as a piece of software for those who prefer an 'off the shelf' approach.

CHAPTER 6

The Behavioral Explorer Assessment System

John Clements and Neil Martin

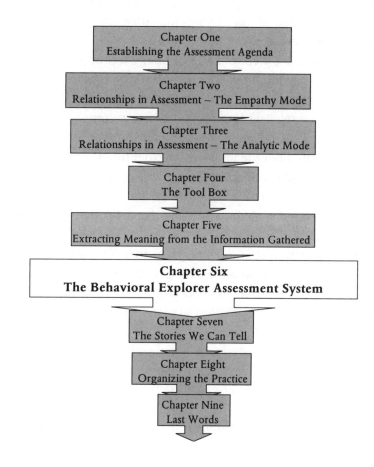

In this chapter we will describe an assessment system designed for people supporting individuals whose behavior is cause for concern. It is an attempt to incorporate many of the ideas that we have discussed in this book into a format that would guide supporters from the first steps of defining a problem through to developing an action plan that would reflect our understanding of that problem. The content reflects the knowledge developed by the empirical psychologies about why people do what they do, but it is designed in a way that makes it accessible to anyone who is interested and motivated. You need not have taken advanced courses in psychology to use the Behavioral Explorer.

The chapter is presented with three outcomes in mind. We hope that it will consolidate what has already been discussed in the book. We hope that it will inspire some readers to design their own systems. For others we hope that it will provide a useful 'off the shelf' tool that will help them get started on developing their interest and skills in behavioral assessment.

The Explorer is a piece of software that is a problem solving guide. In step by step fashion it takes the user through defining the problem, gathering the information that should help make sense of that problem, summarizing the relevant findings, identifying a range of interventions logically related to the analysis and establishing specific action plans linked to some or all of the interventions identified. The Explorer is not a formal psychometric instrument. Technical properties such as reliability have not been investigated. It stands or falls on whether it helps supporters generate action plans that help the individuals they support. At some point, its usefulness in this respect needs to be properly researched. However, it is our judgment that we cannot wait for the research. We think it is important to get such tools into the hands of ordinary practitioners so that we can begin to learn what is helpful and what is not. The present situation in many countries is an urgent one. There are considerable numbers of people with developmental disabilities whose behavior is cause for serious concern and most of these people do not receive adequate support. They are often subject to toxic and restrictive interventions (prescription psychotropics, restraints, grossly impoverished environments and lifestyles). It is important that we move forward in providing more relevant and competent everyday life interventions. If the Explorer helps with this, we will be delighted. At the very least it will generate interesting information that will challenge some of the narrower perspectives taken on behavioral issues.

The Behavioral Explorer – main elements

The system is divided into three main elements – Information Guide, Formulation Guide, Intervention Guide.

1. *Information Guide*

This is the largest element. It covers defining the target behavior, gathering information of relevance about the person and gathering specific information about the behavior that has been identified as the focus of concern. The guide suggests gathering the information in the sequence laid out and at frequent (and clearly defined) points in the guide the user is prompted to transfer some of the information to the Formulation Guide (the transfer is automatic with the software). Thus by the time that the information gathering is completed, the summary of relevant contributors to the behavior has also been completed.

2. *Formulation Guide*

This contains the behavior identified as the focus of concern, the summary of what seem to be the relevant contributors and a section which takes the assessor step by step to the point of specifying the action plans that will be undertaken and how these plans will be monitored.

3. *Intervention Guide*

This is the least developed element in the system. It lists some of the common immediate and short-term contributors to behaviors and against each contributor it offers a series of relevant interventions. Working day in day out with someone it is easy to run out of ideas. The Intervention Guide is meant to help counter such fatigue. It is also intended as an open-ended element, so that users could add in their own ideas of things that they have found useful. In this way a pool of collective wisdom can be developed over time. The pool could reflect the collective wisdom gathered around an individual or gathered by a service. The software may be developed further to actively promote this aspect (see later).

Using the system

Although the system prescribes the sequence of activity in the assessment process, it leaves it open as to how that process is managed. One person could direct and coordinate the whole thing; different parts of the Information Guide could be allocated to different team members; team members could cover the same areas independently and then compare notes to see if they come up with the same information. Where a group of people are involved in doing the assessment and it is difficult to get them all in the same room at the same time, the software will enable people to view/add to/challenge each other's contributions before moving to a consensus view as to both what the facts are and what they mean.

The Information Guide

The Information Guide is divided into three sections:

- Section 1 – Defining the behavior of concern.
- Section 2 – Just who are we talking about?
- Section 3 – So just what is this specific behavior about?

Section 1 – Defining the behavior of concern

This section helps the supporters think through the issues involved in deciding which behaviors justify some kind of planned intervention and, within that group, which behavior will be the specific focus of the present assessment. The users are directed to focus on one specific behavior as the target of assessment, even if there are several behaviors that are justifiable cause for concern. The main part of the section is an open-ended checklist of behaviors that are rated in terms of frequency, intensity, problem to self, problem to others. This part is reproduced in Figure 6.1.

RATING SCALE DEFINITIONS

FREQUENCY
1. Occurs less than once a week
2. Occurs no more than once a week
3. Occurs several times a week but not every day
4. Occurs at least once a day
5. Occurs more than once every day

INTENSITY
1. Behavior is of concern but not threatening or damaging
2. Others feel threatened by the behavior but damage does not occur and upset is not serious
3. Inflicts pain without bruising/breakage of skin. Property is damaged but not destroyed. Upset is significant but not lasting.
4. Inflicts bruising/breakage of skin. Property destroyed. Creates significant upset which damages relationships.
5. Inflicts severe physical damage requiring hospital attendance. Creates widespread property damage. Creates lasting trauma in others.

PROBLEM TO SELF
1. The behavior does not affect ✎   at all
2. The behavior draws attention to ✎   but does not restrict life
3. The behavior limits ✎   's life experiences (for example, not able to go to certain places/activities)
4. ✎   is on a major tranquilizer as a result of the behavior
5. ✎   is permanently damaged physically by the behavior (for example, loss of vision, additional brain damage)

PROBLEM TO OTHERS
1. The behavior does not affect other people at all
2. Others are upset by the behavior when it occurs but not otherwise affected
3. Others are physically damaged or severely upset by the behavior
4. The behavior inflicts longer-term physical and/or emotional damage on others. Their own lives are restricted to some extent.
5. The lives of others are severely restricted by the behavior

BEHAVIOR CHECKLIST

BEHAVIOR	FREQUENCY	INTENSITY	PROBLEM – SELF	PROBLEM – OTHERS
Hits others				
Damages property				
Steals				
Kicks others				
Smears feces				
Sexually assaults others				
Bangs head against surfaces				
Verbally abuses				
Pinches/ scratches others				
Pinches/ scratches self				
Attacks others with weapons				
Exposes genitals				
Bites others				
Bites self				
Screams				
Hits own head				
Tells lies				

Figure 6.1 Behavior rating scale

Having completed the rating scale, users are then guided to identify all the behaviors that are significant enough to justify intervention and then to select one from this list.

Section 2 – Just who are we talking about?

This section tries to ensure that we have some real grasp of the person whose specific behavior we are going to try to change – it is an attempt to 'person center' the behavioral assessment. It is made up of six subsections.

(a)   Where's the individual coming from?
This generates a lifeline from birth to the present, marking in key life events such as changes, losses, traumas, new challenges, illnesses.

(b)   Who are the significant people in the individual's life?
This is a relationship map that puts the person at the center with those involved in her life scattered around. The map details the type of relationship (staff, relative), the closeness of the relationship and the quality of the relationship (positive, negative, mixed).

(c)   What are the important places in the person's life?
The person's current place of residence is at the center, with other places dotted around in a way that indicates which places the person spends most time in.

(d)   The kind of person he is
This is a first view of personality, an area also picked up in Section 3. It consists of a series of descriptive words which are circled if they are felt to apply, with scope for adding important words to the list if need be. There is then a more detailed exploration of core, specific motivations – the specific things that the person takes active steps to obtain and the specific things that he takes active steps to escape from or avoid. A rating scale format is used for this area. A sample is presented in Figure 6.2.

The first part looks at **THE THINGS THAT** ✎   **WORKS TO OBTAIN**

Each item is rated on a 1–5 scale, defined as:

1. Not a motivator at all
2. Seems to like but does not make much effort to get
3. Sometimes works to get
4. Will often make considerable effort to get
5. Nearly always makes a lot of effort to get

You can rate anywhere along the line. For each item that you rate 3 or above try to give specific examples.

SOCIAL CONTACT FROM OTHERS:

1	2	3	4	5

Specific examples:

PRAISE:

1	2	3	4	5

Specific examples:

FOOD ITEMS:

1	2	3	4	5

Specific examples:

DRINKS:

1	2	3	4	5

Specific examples:

CIGARETTES:

1	2	3	4	5

Specific examples:

SEXUAL STIMULATION:

1	2	3	4	5

Specific examples:

OTHER FORMS OF SENSORY STIMULATION:

1	2	3	4	5

Specific examples:

ACCESS TO LEISURE ACTIVITIES:

1	2	3	4	5

Specific examples:

OTHER (any other item/event/activity not included above – please specify what this is):

1	2	3	4	5

Specific examples:

Figure 6.2 Assessment of core motivations

(e)   Personal competence resources

This examines in detail the person's functioning in the areas that relate most closely to behavioral difficulties. The assessment looks at the main communicative messages that the person puts out and how these are conveyed, the emotions that he exhibits, their dominance and how strong feelings are managed by the individual, the sorts of activities that the person can engage in without support and the competence that the person shows in understanding the social world. Figure 6.3 illustrates the assessment of emotions. Figure 6.4 details the assessment of social understanding.

(f)   Health issues

This provides a checklist of common health issues, which can be added to and which are rated in terms of whether they are a current, recurrent or past problem.

Section 3 – So just what is this specific behavior about?

This section turns to examining in detail the specific focus of concern and the likely contributors to that behavior. Having taken a broad look at the person and her circumstances this is now a fine-grained assessment of the specific behavior. This analysis is divided into the three time frames – immediate influences, short-term influences and longer-term influences.

For the immediate and short-term influences, the Explorer system offers a choice of analytic tools. One tool is a series of rating scales that tap the knowledge of those very familiar with the person and the behavior. Specific possible contributors are listed and rated for their link to the behavior in question. Such ratings cover events before incidents, events after incidents and short-term influences (as detailed earlier in this text). Figure 6.5 illustrates the format.

Now we are looking at the feelings that we see ✎ expressing. This is a difficult area because it can be very hard to make sense of what another person is feeling. The assessment summarizes the information in a table with four columns. In the *first column* goes the emotion that is expressed – some common emotion words are provided. The person may not show all of these, so do not feel that you have to rate each one. You may feel that other words better describe the emotions that ✎ shows – feel free to change or add words. In the *second column* goes a description of what ✎ does when feeling that way – how the feeling is expressed. In the *third column* goes information about the events or experiences that trigger the emotion, bring out the feeling. If you do not know the answer, say so (Not Known). In the *fourth column* rate the frequency with which each emotion is shown - use a 1–3 scale (1 – Occasionally, 2 –- Quite often, 3 – Frequently).

EMOTION	HOW EXPRESSED	WHAT TRIGGERS	FREQUENCY
Happy			
Angry			
Tense			
Excited			
Sad			
Embarrassed			
Relaxed			
Sexually aroused			

Figure 6.3 Assessment of general emotional functioning

This section looks at important areas of understanding that help us to inhibit our impulses to act in ways that give rise to concern in others. It is about the capacity of the individual to understand and be sensitive to the thoughts and feelings of others and to understand the longer-term consequences of actions. This again is a crude attempt to assess a complicated area. It uses rating scales to assess statements about social understanding. The ratings are as follows:

1.   Not true at all
2.   True to a small extent
3.   True to some extent
4.   Quite true
5.   Very true

The individual can resist 'temptation' even when not under direct supervision. There are things that the individual likes to do but these things are not allowed. The individual avoids doing these things when others are supervising, but the rating here is about whether they also avoid doing these things when there is no one supervising:

1	2	3	4	5

The individual shows some genuine remorse or concern after doing something that is hurtful or damaging to another:

1	2	3	4	5

The individual is kind to animals and handles them in a gentle way:

1	2	3	4	5

The individual demonstrates the ability to adjust emotions and behavior to the states that other people are in – he shows some concern when others are hurt or unhappy, shows pleasure when others are happy/excited:

1	2	3	4	5

The individual demonstrates the capacity to think ahead and to avoid doing things that will lead to trouble later:

1	2	3	4	5

The individual has a sense of property ownership – things that are her own, things that belong to others – and demonstrates respect for the property of others:

1	2	3	4	5

Figure 6.4 The assessment of social understanding

In many service settings these factors will be assessed by incident records. The Explorer package also includes a recording form that can be used if a service does not already have one available (see Chapter 4). The software package offers the option of a rapid and highly structured recording of each incident directly into the system with the analysis automated and updated after each entry. The assessment of short-term influences also includes a version of the three questions exercise mentioned in Chapter 4.

The assessment of longer-term influences is more tentative and acknowledges the need for more specialized assessments in this area. However, the Explorer system does include the job aids detailed in this text (Chapter 4) for assessing social system characteristics and personality. It also uses the quality of life domains to encourage consideration of broader environmental characteristics that may be playing a role in the behavior of concern. Life events were already covered in Section 2.

Because of the regular prompts to transfer specified information to the Formulation Guide, by the time that the Information Guide is completed, the core of the Formulation Guide will also be completed.

These are events that occur just before the behavior itself. Rate these events using a 5-point scale:

1. Never occurs before the behavior
2. Occasionally occurs before the behavior (no more than 10% of incident records note this event)
3. Sometimes occurs before the behavior (mentioned in 10–25% of incident recordings)
4. Often occurs before the behavior (mentioned in 25–50% of incident recordings)
5. Very frequently occurs before the behavior (mentioned in more than 50% of incident recordings)

Food or drink is present or is being prepared:

        1   2   3   4   5

✎ **is asked to do something (carry out a task of some sort):**

        1   2   3   4   5

A particular individual is present or enters the room:

        1   2   3   4   5

✎ **is told that he cannot have or do something:**

        1   2   3   4   5

There has been no social contact/attention given to ✎   for several minutes:

        1   2   3   4   5

✎   **has not been involved in a task or activity for several   minutes: has been the target of teasing or verbal abuse:**

1   2   3   4   5

✎   **has been involved in an argument:**

1   2   3   4   5

Something that ✎   **is known to be sensitive to occurred (for example, a noise, a word, physical contact, seeing/hearing a dog):**
Please describe here what exactly the sensitivity is…

1   2   3   4   5

OTHER:

Please list here other events that occur before incidents and rate each one on the 1–5 scale as above.

Figure 6.5 Assessing immediate influences - events before an incident

The Formulation Guide

The Formulation Guide at first follows the sequence of the Information Guide. It starts with the behavior that has been defined as the focus of assessment. It then has selected information from the 'Just who are we talking about?' section:

- life events in the last five years and trauma experienced at any time
- words used to describe the person

- the main general motivations of the individual
- the main topics of communication
- the most prominent emotions displayed
- the individual's tactics for managing strong emotions
- activities that engage the individual independently for ten minutes or more
- social thinking capabilities
- health issues.

The next section summarizes the specific factors identified as influencing the occurrence of the behavior in question. This is reproduced in Figure 6.6. This section also includes the summary of the things that are thought to support or promote positive functioning.

The second half of the Formulation Guide is a series of prompts to help those involved translate the summary of what has been learned into real world action plans. The prompts are:

- Re-read the first part of the Formulation Guide.
- Put into your own words the main reasons for the behavior of concern.
- Put into your own words the things that help the person cope without engaging in the behavior.
- Identify new skills that would help the person function more positively more often.
- Read again the whole Formulation Guide to this point.
- Brainstorm ideas that would help the person engage in the behavior of concern much less often.
- List those ideas that will definitely be turned into action plans.
- Identify who needs to do what by when to make those action plans happen.

The Formulation Guide closes with a prompt to make sure that there is in place a behavior monitoring system for judging as objectively as possible whether the action plans are actually impacting the behavior.

SO JUST WHAT IS THIS SPECIFIC BEHAVIOR ABOUT?

LONGER-TERM INFLUENCES

SHORT-TERM INFLUENCES

IMMEDIATE INFLUENCES – Events before an incident

BEHAVIOR

IMMEDIATE INFLUENCES – Events after an incident

And we also need to remind ourselves that the following things SUPPORT OR PROMOTE POSITIVE FUNCTIONING

Figure 6.6 Formulation Guide layout for summarizing key contributors to behavioral incidents

The Intervention Guide

This is the least developed part of the Explorer System and the one that is designed to be open-ended, so that users can readily add interventions that have proved useful. It focuses only on some of the immediate and short-term influences and tries to illustrate interventions that would logically follow from identifying a specific contributory factor in the assessment. Figure 6.7 shows the layout. It is not meant as a 'treatment manual'. It is meant as a help to people working with the individual day in day out who may have got stuck for ideas, or for people who are not fully familiar with assessment and how it can be linked to intervention.

Although this is the smallest and least developed element in the system, field trials have suggested it as a very popular element and one where there could be some very profitable sharing between practitioners. At the time of writing there are plans to attempt to coordinate the ideas and experiences of practitioners on helpful interventions at the website through which the Explorer software is marketed. In time this might lead to a continually updated and downloadable element to the system.

INTERVENTION IDEAS FOR IDENTIFIED TRIGGERS/ANTECEDENTS

IDENTIFIED CONTRIBUTOR	INTERVENTION IDEAS
Presence of food/drink	Give more access (ST)
	Set up visual communication system to help understanding of when food/drink available (MT)
	Teach communication skill to request items (MT–LT)
	Teach how to help self or prepare food/drinks (MT–LT)
Presence of specific person	Keep the two apart (ST)
	Alter how the other responds to the behavior (ST–MT)
	Teach a social/communication skill to get the desired response from the other (MT–LT)*
Request/instruction	Avoid demand (ST)
	Alter how request/instruction presented (ST–MT)
	Sequence a favorite activity to follow problematic request (MT)
	Put the problematic request in the middle of a sequence of requests with which the person is known to cooperate (ST–MT)
	Set up visual communication system to indicate what follows the requested activity (MT)
	Use a timer to indicate when an activity will end (ST–MT)*
	Directly reinforce cooperation (ST–MT)*
	Teach skill to request 'No', 'Finish', 'Break' (MT–LT)*

ST, MT, LT – short term, medium term, long term. Crude estimate of time needed to judge impact of intervention on a target behavior (defined more fully in the guide itself).

* Indicates interventions for which the advice and support of a qualified professional (for example, psychologist, communications therapist) should be sought.

Figure 6.7 Extract from the Intervention Guide

Concluding remarks

Time will tell if the Explorer system proves a useful tool for practitioners. Even if it fails, it is our hope that something better will come in its place, but that something has to be accessible to ordinary people trying to help people with disabilities get on with their lives. Everybody knows something about human behavior. Academic psychology has made a valuable but small contribution to the accumulated wisdom about why people do what they do. It is important not to let this accumulated psychological knowledge become the sole property of highly trained and expensive experts and consultants. Not only is this to practice a deception – that to understand people you need at least seven years' university level training – but it is also to guarantee that people with disabilities with serious behavioral issues will not access the highest quality of personal supports. There will simply not be enough 'experts', let alone the money to pay them. The tools of psychology have to be in the hands of those involved with the individual on a day-to-day basis. This means that they must be accessible to those people. Access should not be denied either by language (technical jargon/psychobabble) or by the restrictive business practices of professional guilds. All that is known about applied psychology can be made accessible to all those who need to know. We hope that the Explorer system makes a contribution but its shortcomings should not obscure the real heart of the enterprise – access to knowledge and the provision of supports that are woven into the fabric of everyday life.

CHAPTER 7

The Stories We Can Tell

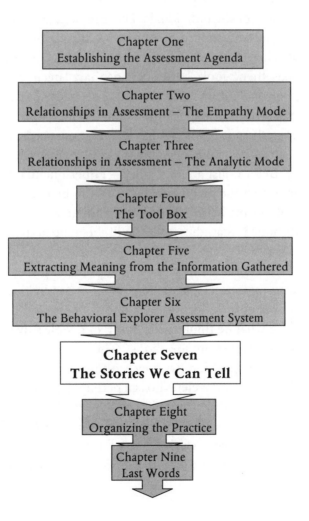

Chapter One
Establishing the Assessment Agenda

Chapter Two
Relationships in Assessment – The Empathy Mode

Chapter Three
Relationships in Assessment – The Analytic Mode

Chapter Four
The Tool Box

Chapter Five
Extracting Meaning from the Information Gathered

Chapter Six
The Behavioral Explorer Assessment System

**Chapter Seven
The Stories We Can Tell**

Chapter Eight
Organizing the Practice

Chapter Nine
Last Words

Much of this book has been devoted to the information that we need to collect and the tools that can help us to collect it successfully when we are seeking to understand better the reasons why behaviors occur. However, we have also tried to explore what is perhaps the most challenging area – what you do with the information gathered, how you weave it into a plausible 'story' that has testable implications. Chapter 6 began this effort, which is continued here and, to a lesser extent, in the next chapter.

The present chapter reproduces three assessment reports that one of the authors (JC) has written in the last few years. These reports are reproduced courtesy of the parents, who had the legal authority to give consent on behalf of the individuals. These reports are not put forward as 'perfect' in any way. Indeed on re-reading them many shortcomings are apparent. They have not, however, been amended in any significant way to make them look better (typos have been corrected and identifying personal information altered). The reader has, by and large, the documents that those supporting the individuals have. The purpose of reproducing them is to show how information can be combined to create a human story – an understandable and, in many ways, ordinary human story. But not just a pretty story – rather one that has practical implications so that the quality of the story can be judged by whether those implications prove of benefit to the individual. By reading these stories it is hoped that the reader will be helped to see how to summarize assessment information in an accessible and functional way. In Chapter 8 we continue this process by reproducing specific behavior plans linked to these assessments (for two of the individuals).

The reports also reflect things about their author – current perspectives on what he thinks he is doing in people's lives, issues that were considered earlier in this book. The move is away from the professional/expert position, with everything done in a standardized way, towards the fellow traveler who can perhaps help to guide the party through the present difficult terrain but who is also on a journey – a separate journey. In older traditions, one way that travelers relate to each other is by telling stories – stories that offer not just diversion but also insight and understanding. So, in the spirit of *The Canterbury Tales*, we begin!

Jack The Lad's Tale

Jack is a young man in his mid 20s who lives in his own home with 24-hour staff support (Supported Living). He is limited in his ability to take care of himself and is legally conserved by his father. Since the time of the assessment I have remained as part of the team working to support Jack. Technically I am the behavior consultant to the supported living agency (Beacon). This was my initial assessment report.

Purpose of this assessment

I was asked to provide a perspective upon the needs of Mr Lad, particularly those implicated in the behavioral and emotional difficulties that he presents and experiences. The request came from his father and from Beacon Services. Funding support came from the Regional Center.

As I have got to know Mr Lad quite well over the last year, I feel it not inappropriate to refer to him in this report as Jack.

Methods of work

In the fall of 98 I became involved in the work to support Jack. I have spent time with him at home and met regularly with his father and the support team managed by Beacon Services. I have read and annotated the extensive reports available from his father covering the period 1976 – 1998. I have attended multidisciplinary meetings at Asbury Arts Center and a psychiatric consultation at the Regional Center.

In addition, for the specific purpose of preparing this report I have:

- content analyzed the staff logs kept by those who support Jack at home for the period December 98 through October 99

- got those who know Jack well in his home-setting to complete elements from the Behavioral Explorer package

- spent additional time with Jack

- met with the Program Director at Asbury Arts Center and reviewed the data available there, covering the time that Jack has used the service.

The behaviors of concern

Jack can do a number of things that cause concern in others. On occasions he can strike at himself, bang his head against solid surfaces, destroy property and hurt others (hit, kick, bite, head-butt, pinch, scratch). He does not do these things often. There are phases when he does them more often and more intensely and he can put himself and others at risk for significant injury. Significant damage to property can also occur, both at his own home and in other people's cars. Mostly, but not always, these overt behaviors are accompanied by heightened arousal and negatively toned feelings.

Building an understanding

WIDE ANGLE

The journey

What follows is a brief summary of what we understand to be the major events in Jack's life:

1976	Jack born (July 1st)
1980	Sara, his sister, born
1983	Jim, his brother, born
1989	Jack moves out of the family home to live at Knottvery Developmental Center. He is subject to repeated assaults, some serious
1991	Moves to live in foster home
1992	Jack's mother starts to become ill
1993	Jack's mother in car wreck
1995	Jack's mother dies
1995	Jack moves to new foster home
1997	Jack moves to own home
1999	Crisis leads to temporary hospitalization

Jack is a young man. Since his early adolescence he has had a traumatic life. This sequence of events is bound to take its toll, and stability in a high quality life is an essential part of the healing process.

The man

CORE CHARACTERISTICS

When I asked those who know him well to identify key characteristics that they associate with Jack, there was very limited overlap in the words chosen. I suspect that getting close to the real man is a considerable challenge. There are clear and defining characteristics but the elements are perhaps a little at variance with each other, not quite what we would expect to go together, not fitting any stereotyped mold.

The core characteristics that emerge from all the material available to me include the following.

Jack is generally an energetic person and a great socializer. He is an active communicator, using a range of media (speech, gestures, behavior) and covering a range of topics (mainly personal preferences and current feelings). He likes and charms a lot of people and although he is not great with changes in his life, somehow the arrival of attractive women into his circle seems to cause little trauma. He enjoys relating to a wide range of people. He is a bit over the top in how he presents to others – a bit noisy, a bit of a joker, a 'real tease' (Francis, at Asbury). In British slang, we might refer to him as 'Jack the lad'. However he is not one to be messed with – he is very determined to do things his way and is not great at accepting compromise, correction or direct instruction. His cooperation has to be won.

He is also an immensely sensual person – he loves to be tickled and massaged, he loves fooling around in the bath and pool, he loves animals of many kinds, he loves elaborate visual stimulation (cartoons and books, his own self-generated stimulation), he relates to a range of music and music exerts a noticeable effect on his mood, he loves his food, he is sexually active. The sensual life is much more where he is at than any kind of learning – he has never shown much interest in learning to do things for himself or at doing school type tasks. He is a lotus-eater, not much troubled by ambition or guilt.

However, he can learn around areas important to him – he loves animals but could certainly be rather rough with them. In the last year he has grasped the need to be gentle with the dogs in his circle (Michelle's Lucky and Marlene's Kodiak). Yet one wonders if there is a price for this core element of his make up – presumably such a sensory focus means that aches, pains and other discomforts are that much more intense.

And intensity is a word that begins to emerge in trying to get to grips with Jack. He is not really a laid back person – he is intensely discriminating. He knows who likes him and who does not, hates it when people talk about him in front of him, has a good eye for an attractive woman; he is choosy about what he eats and does not eat, who comes into his home, what he looks at, what he listens to and when he listens to it (he will match music to mood to some extent) and who he mixes with. He associates individual people with specific activities, not really wanting to do the same things with everyone. He is sensitive to and often dislikes changes in his routines. He is not that easily pleased – his likes and dislikes are intense and he is not really accommodating to the issues of other people.

Thus we have a charming, sociable, sensual, discriminating, intense person...hard to sum up in a single word!

UPS AND DOWNS

The notion of 'phases' has long been around Jack. In 1982 he was noted to go through phases of eating well and eating less. In 1985 there was mention of phases when he showed more or less interest in activities. His level of communicativeness and particularly his use of words have fluctuated. It is not clear from the records whether these kinds of phases coincided with fluctuations in emotional and behavioral functioning.

Overt behavioral difficulties were not present in the first few years of life. In his early years Jack did have mobility problems (as he has now), was always difficult to motivate to do things for himself and was rather stubborn. However, he seemed a generally happy child. Around 1984 this seemed to change and aggression, self-injury and property damage started to be noted. These behaviors have remained part of how Jack presents himself, right up to the present day, but they have run a fluctuating course. The fluctuations have been linked to environmental changes, the sorts of major life changes described above. Indeed the onset of these difficulties was linked to the birth of Jack's brother Jim, and Jim was always a target for Jack's aggression. I would urge caution with such an interpretation as such onsets can occur around this age without a major life event and, as we have learned subsequently, phases can occur in the absence of major life changes. Thus, although it has become part of the received wisdom around Jack that he does not like change and that major changes can trigger phases of significant emotional and behavioral difficulties, it has now become clear that there may be other factors at work in precipitating difficult times – the crisis earlier this year certainly occurred at a time of apparent stability in his environment.

Although phases have long been noted, most reports covering Jack's childhood and adolescence refer to him as a healthy person. It is only in 1996 that reports start to refer to a very significant physical health dimension to the phases. At this time, phases seem to include factors such as loss of appetite, low energy, weight loss, sleep problems, dehydration. More recently additional health issues, especially around bowel functioning, skin irritation and headaches, have also been implicated and he has been found to be intolerant to quite a wide range of medications. The most recent crisis (spring 99) involved behavioral, emotional and physical health issues and occurred at a time of environmental stability and good quality of life.

Thus there are the long-term, fundamental features that help us to understand in general who Jack is and the kind of life that will work for him. Yet every so often he gets downed, he hits a wall, and every kind of system is now implicated – his health, his sleep, his emotions, his behavior, his communication – he becomes for a time a different person. He has some kind of vulnerability. It can be activated by major life stressors but it is now clear that there are other factors at work. At this stage we are not sure how to characterize those factors or how to characterize the crisis itself (see below). The last two difficult phases have occurred in the springtime (March–May period).

ZOOMING IN

Life now

Jack lives in his own home. People come in to provide support to him and the relationships so forged are strong, positive and, in many cases, enduring. His father remains closely involved, as do his siblings. For weekday activities he receives support from a skilled and innovative agency that facilitate his access to a range of activities. Jack has a lot of control in his life and a lot of fans – this suits him just fine.

Personal priorities

As described above, Jack is a man of strong views with a clear understanding of what he likes and does not like. Work on his person centered plan is nearing completion and this will provide much more specific and detailed information about preferences.

However, the analysis of the common themes around which he initiates communication certainly helps us to understand the priority issues for Jack. Those who support him at home see the main issues about which he initiates communication to be:

- wants – food, activities, interaction, bed, diaper changing
- don't wants – activities/task, people being around him (own space wanted).

All these things are usually communicated by understandable words and gestures.

- Physical discomfort – around bowels, head (?aches) or skin.

This is usually communicated by behavior such as banging walls, hitting himself or banging his head.

In terms of his general emotional functioning, those who support him see a range of emotions. The most common emotions are positive – happy, excited, relaxed. Negative emotions are seen, but less frequently. He will become angry if he does not get what he wants. He does also seem to be tense and sad on occasions (he even cries sometimes) but the causes of these feelings are not understood by those who know him well.

The above descriptions refer to how Jack is most of the time. He does get into crisis when he is less communicative and more predominantly in a distressed state. This will be considered later.

Behaviors of concern – searching for meaning

The main analysis is based upon the logs kept by the staff who support Jack at home. An 11-month period was analyzed.

The behaviors noted most frequently in the logs were banging walls and hitting himself. Incidents of aggression to others, throwing things, banging his head against a solid surface, spitting and tearing things are much less commonly noted. The cross tabs of behaviors and a range of possible associated factors showed one very clear 'cluster' – high levels of general movement, high levels of stereotypy, high levels of agitation and self-hitting. Bowel problems were noted most commonly in association with this cluster. Banging walls clustered with lots of movement and agitation. Aggression did not show such clear clustering.

When incidents were broken down by time of day, most of the behaviors that give rise to concern seem more likely to happen in the afternoon or evening. Mornings seem generally more positive times. This association was most marked for aggression and least for self-hitting.

The details are presented in an Appendix to this report.

It was not possible to analyze the data at Asbury in the same way. From a reading of the file, the picture above is generally confirmed although the link with am/pm may not be as clear as it appears from the tables in the Appendix. Aggression is much less common than self-injury but is probably noted more often than in the home logs.

On the basis of the present data there look to be at least two distinct sets of issues:

1. There is a generally aroused state, marked by agitation, stereotypy, self-hitting and wall banging. This can occur at any time, although more often later in the day, and tends to be associated with bowel issues, usually constipation.

2. Aggression seems separable from this cluster and its meaning is not clear from the present data. However, the association with time of day suggests a possible role for lowered mood and lack of energy (normal biorhythms) but clearly there must be other factors. At least one of those is physical intervention when Jack is injuring himself but there may be other factors. In other words aggression may or may not be part of the same response class as self-injury – the present data do not permit a firm conclusion.

Other behaviors occurred too rarely for any hypotheses to be drawn.

Putting it all together – making sense of the behavioral issues?

At this stage, no clear interpretation emerges for behaviors that are aggressive to others. These behaviors may be separate from the other behaviors of concern and will need more specific assessment in their own right.

What does seem clear is that some incidents of all the behaviors in question suggest a clear communicative function – Jack is a very strong-minded person with strong preferences and if things are not going as he wants them, he can communicate this directly through behavior. He can also communicate about these issues by words and gestures but his communicative competence does fluctuate over time. Thus it may well be that he is more likely to communicate through behavior when he is having difficulty with his words. This is evident in his clear down phases but he may also have more difficulty when he is tired (hence the greater likelihood of incidents later in the day, when mood and energy levels tend to be lower).

General arousal level seems to have a role to play – there is tentative evidence that if Jack is excited for any reason this may increase the likelihood of both aggression and self-injury. Such a phenomenon is not unusual.

A third and key contributor, particularly to self-hitting, is a loss of well-being. This shows up in day-to-day fluctuations and also at the crisis phases. There are often physical health issues such as constipation and the behaviors are usually accompanied by agitation, high rates of movement and stereotypy. Whilst these factors can come and go on a day-to-day basis, in the crisis phase they are more pervasive, the behaviors increase in severity and frequency and additional systems become involved (loss of sleep, loss of appetite, loss of communications skills). At present we have no clear understanding of the nature of the crisis phase. There are several possible ways to think about it:

1. The crisis is one of physical health – for example, an undiagnosed bowel or neurological disorder.

2. The crisis is one of mental health – an affective disorder (bi or uni polar), a schizophrenic disorder, a post traumatic stress disorder or a severe grief reaction (the last two major down

phases have occurred around the anniversary of his mother's death).

3. A whole new field is emerging that reveals complex interplays between environment, health and neurological functioning. So, for example, in the field of autism there is speculation and some research to indicate that people with this label may have gut related problems (leaky guts and problems with metabolizing gluten and casein) that lead to intermittent flooding of the brain with peptides of the opiate type. There is research in schizophrenia around the role of retroviruses in precipitating breakdown. There is the work around the difficulties faced by some Gulf War veterans.

At this stage it is important to keep our minds open to all these possibilities.

Although we have as yet no clear model for understanding the crises that Jack experiences, we know enough about some of the issues to take practical steps that may reduce the likelihood or severity of future crises and that will minimize the day-to-day behavioral issues. These will be spelled out in the next section.

The implications for supporting Mr Lad

The above analysis has the following practical implications:

1. There is a need to share this assessment with Jack's medical practitioners, to see if any further physical investigations are merited at this stage.

2. There is a need to respect Jack's clear and appropriate expression of his preferences. This is generally understood by all those who support Jack at present.

3. Given the role of communication and fluctuating functioning in this area, there is a need for a comprehensive 'back up' system of visual communication to enable Jack to express his preferences even if he is having difficulty with his words. This development is already under way.

4. There is a gap in Jack's formal communication skills about his own internal states (particularly head and stomach discomfort). There is a need to develop his skills in this area.

5. Jack loves massage and has learned to be gentle around animals. This indicates a possibility for teaching him more gentle ways to manage the discomforts that he experiences (self-massage not self-injury).

6. Given the uncertain nature of the crises that Jack experiences, it is worthwhile considering interventions that promote or sustain balance and harmony. Jack loves massage and he has in his circle someone skilled in this area. We will therefore draw upon this to develop a massage routine targeted at promoting balance and harmony. This can be taught to all those supporting Jack so that he can have input of this kind every day. Care will be taken to manage any boundary issues – the targeted areas are likely to be hands, feet, neck and shoulders.

7. Jack has had a traumatic past and this will contribute to some of the behavioral difficulties. The practical implications are that we should:

    • maintain his general quality of life, with control being a very central issue for him

    • prepare him for changes and develop life story materials for him (some work has already been done on this)

    • offer reassurance at times when he appears anxious or sad

    • avoid exposure to people who might aggress upon him.

8. Although we do not understand fully the crises, we have learned a lot about the sequence of events and can therefore plan to adjust our support as we identify the build up. This may avoid crises developing and will enable us to deal competently with those that we do not prevent. This planning has already been undertaken.

9. There is need for further assessment work on behaviors that are targeted to others and I will discuss with the support team how this might be undertaken.

Concluding remarks

Getting close to understanding Jack is a tremendous challenge – at one level a lot is known about him but there is something elusive about who he really is and what some of his needs are. I hope that this assessment has provided some ideas that are useful to informing the support that we provide to Jack. However, it is obvious to me that there is much still to be learned.

Appendix

Table 7.1: Data from the analysis of the staff logs December 98–October 99	
BEHAVIOR	**MENTIONS**
Banging walls	17
Hitting self	15
Aggression to others	6
Throwing things	2
Banging head to surface	1
Spitting	1
Tearing things	1

Table 7.2: Behavior related to time of day							
	BANG WALLS	HIT SELF	AGGRESSION	THROW	HEAD TO SURFACE	SPIT	TEAR
AM	5	7 (5)	0	0	0	0	0
PM	12	8 (10)	6	2	1	1	1

Note

For 'Hit Self' there were two incidents when the time of day was uncertain. Thus the two figures illustrate allocation to morning or afternoon.

Table 7.3: Behavior related to associated conditions						
	BANG WALLS	HIT SELF	AGGRESSION	THROW	HEAD TO SURFACE	SPIT	TEAR
Bowels	0	4	1	0	0	0	0
Other ill	0	0	0	0	0	0	0
Hi Move	6	6	1	0	0	0	0
Hi Stereos	0	7	1	0	0	0	0
Crying	0	0	1	0	0	0	0
Agitation	8	8	2	2	0	0	1
Happy	1	1	2	0	0	0	1
Hi Eat	0	1	0	0	0	0	0
Lo Eat	0	0	0	0	0	1	0
Talkative	1	3	0	0	0	0	0
Headache	1	2	0	0	0	0	0

Update to the time of writing the book

A detailed plan was developed linking 'stages' of functioning to what staff did to support Jack on a day-to-day basis. Jack had a sustained, positive phase in his life lasting 12–18 months. There was no crisis period, all the behaviors of concern were at a low level, there was a close-knit group supporting Jack, and his general quality of life was excellent. Some of the implications spelled out in the report were implemented, some not and some were tried but did not work out. In mid 2000 an attempt was made to alter Jack's medication – this did not work out and Jack became less stable. There then followed a disastrous sequence of events. A dystonic reaction was misdiagnosed in an ER as a seizure and there then followed several attempts to try anti-convulsants, all of which adversely affected Jack, behaviorally and emotionally. There were major changes in the staff supporting Jack. Finally the suspicions of a major physical health difficulty were confirmed. Jack's quality of life collapsed – he refused to leave his house, became less and less cooperative, more and more obsessed around specific things and increasingly disturbed in his behavior. At present we are working on all fronts to sustain his support network and reconnect him to his life. We are seeing some success with this. The behavioral component is focused on managing the aggression (which has been subject to the additional analysis recommended in the report). The behavior plan is included in Chapter 8.

The Maid's Tale

Marian is a woman in her mid 30s whom I was asked to assess as a 'one off'. Her support systems were stuck and were looking for some fresh insights/directions. Marian lived in the community in a group home and attended a day program for people identified as having developmental disabilities. I have not remained involved with Marian although I hear of her from time to time.

Purpose of consultation

I was asked by Valley Support Services (VSS) to provide an assessment input that would help to illuminate Ms 's general needs and more specifically to throw light upon a behavior causing current concern: spending excessive amounts of time in the bathroom. This referral was agreed to by Ms's conservator who is her mother.

Methods of work

I reviewed documentation held on file at VSS. I met with Ms on two occasions at her home and spent time in conversation with her and generally joining in activities. I gathered information from discussions with IT (Program Director), E and O (Support Workers) at VSS, from BM, Program Director at Bayhouse and from Ms's mother.

At my initial meeting with Ms I asked whether she preferred that I called her Marian or Ms. She said that she preferred Marian and I will refer to her thus in the rest of this report.

Outline of the present report

The report is divided into 4 parts:

1. **Marian's story?** An attempt to integrate the information gathered into a story that tries to make sense of the many facets that Marian presents to those who are involved with her.

2. **Long-term needs identified and the action implications.** Drawing, from the story, a list of specific needs and how those might be addressed. Some of these involve

major lifestyle issues; others are more about everyday ways of working.

3. **Working with Marian when she has lost her overall sense of well-being**. Marian goes through crises and this section will comment on some of the things to do when she is struggling to feel OK.

4. **Concluding remarks.**

Marian's story?

Marian is her parents' first-born child. She was recognized from her early years as a child with developmental disabilities that were pervasive. Although much of her formal education took place in special education settings, for most of her school life these settings were physically located in mainstream neighborhood schools. Thus to varying degrees she spent time with the other children of her age and grew up in much the same way as they did – living at home, going to her local school, going out and about in her local community.

There are certain personal characteristics that run through Marian's development. Spoken language has never been that friendly a medium for her – she has progressed well but it has taken a lot of effort on her part and the competence she has gained may mask to others some of the underlying thinking difficulties that she has. She has probably relied a lot on learning things by heart without always understanding them and has never really been a fluent conversationalist. Marian has always been interested in social relationships and throughout her life has given clear evidence of a preference to associate with others who are not publicly identified as 'disabled'. She also seems more interested in female companionship. However, she has always struggled with the subtleties of social interaction – she does not seem to read social situations and the thoughts and feelings of others that well, so that she has tended to relate to others in ways that they find hard to take to. Thus it has been difficult for Marian to make friends in her own right and she has often been seen as something of a loner.

Marian has also always been something of a collector – stickers, cards, rocks – the focus has varied but the theme sustains. She is also a documenter, developing scrapbooks, copy writing lots of things out. She has seemed to struggle in the realm of imagination and works much better in visual, concrete media. She has always thrived on structure and had difficulty in coping with changes in routine. Her grasp of time lapse and sequence has been uncertain, so that she tends to be very fixed in orienting around certain key times and dates – from the time for lunch to the date of her birthday. Those who know her well have learned to adapt to this by not giving her too long a warning about important upcoming events as this tends to make her overly focused on this event. She becomes ever more excited or anxious until her arousal interferes with the event itself (for example, the build up to family occasions leading to her 'zoning out' once the occasion actually arrives).

Marian has always had a tremendously caring side to her. She has always loved looking after animals, shows care and concern for small children and the elderly and indeed had quite a successful spell of working as a volunteer in a child care setting soon after she left school. As a child at home she was always keen to help out with household chores, although this particular interest has waned in her adult life (!). Marian has always been concerned about her own health and focused a lot on physical ailments of one kind or another.

Marian has always had an issue about managing adequately her self-care skills. This seems to reflect some sort of perceptual problem that makes it hard for her to manage 'on the body skills' – it is not because she is lazy.

Thus Marian comes up to school leaving, thriving on the structure that school offers, living a life close to that of other girls of her age and finally having made some real friends at school, particularly Tessa. Her dreams, insofar as they were known, were similar to those of other young women.

The entry to adult life proved traumatic to the point that it has seemed to overwhelm her coping resources. At first things went well but at the age of 20 she had her first major breakdown and since that time there have been cycles of things going well and times when Marian seems to lose her sense of well-being, become more focused on specific topics and act in a variety of ways that others find very frustrating. Why so? We move here from facts to interpretation. What I am seeing from the information available is that...

In adult life Marian's world became more and more unlike the world of the other young women that she grew up with and with whom she identified. As they went off to college, formed relationships, started their own families, moved away from the area, she did not. The few friends that she had made, she lost contact with. Now more of her world was disability focused – she was supported and had formal contact with people not identified as disabled but there was probably less informal contact and she was now very much defined in terms of disability. She found it hard to find satisfactory roles and a personally meaningful lifestyle as a young woman. In addition, adult life tends to be far less structured than school life and exposes more directly any limitations that you have in understanding how the world works. Tolerance shifts as well and so behaviors that people once accepted would now be the target for criticism. When you put these issues together with important life events (the loss of people close to you such as Tessa, the death of a woman at the home where you volunteer, moving away from your family home, women to whom you are close having babies) and whatever personal vulnerability Marian carries for loss of well-being, it perhaps becomes clearer why things have turned out as they have done.

As well as the specific cycles mentioned above I would also add the following interpretations. In many ways Marian has not made the transition to adulthood and has remained in her childhood – doing the puzzles and worksheets that were part of the best time of her life. Indeed she seems to have sabotaged any attempt to move her into adulthood – whenever she looks like succeeding (for example, in work situations or at college) things go wrong…it seems too dangerous to go forward knowing that your real dreams may never be fulfilled, so you go back. When you have gone back you are angry, very angry, and seek to take this out on others; you do the things that get them very angry. This is not best represented by saying that your specific behaviors are 'attention seeking' – rather you seek a social response from others that matches your own feeling state…you want them to be angry and frustrated too.

This is a story – one possible interpretation of the factual information available to me. It has many specific implications for what we see as Marian's needs and the actions needed to meet those needs. If we take those actions and things get better, then to some extent the story is validated. If we take those actions and things do not get better, then the interpretations will need to be reviewed.

Long-term needs identified and the action implications

- **Need:** *Marian needs an adult lifestyle that works for her*

Whilst it will take time to flesh out all the details of this, a number of broad-brush statements can be made. Marian needs to find a life as a woman who does not have children and we need to think about role models that we could expose her to. Marian shows clearly that she prefers to associate with more articulate people, especially if they are not officially identified as disabled, and therefore her lifestyle needs to help her to access these kinds of relationships as much as possible. In the past getting Marian into employment situations has not proved very successful and although this should be a long-term goal it would not be something to work on right now. Likewise I would counsel caution about continuing education at this stage until we are clearer about the role it might play in developing Marian's chosen lifestyle. Instead I would see the first focus to be upon active leisure (hiking and tennis) and volunteering (using either Marian's caring strengths in relation to animals or humans, or her clerical strengths in assembling and copying). At some point we need to consider Marian's living arrangements but until we feel more confident that we are on the right track with Marian we should not see this as an immediate priority. What is a priority is to minimize her exposure to the things that she finds unsatisfactory about her current living situation.

Table 7.4: First of the action implications for Marian

---

1. We need to arrange services so that we are building a life for Marian that works for her, with the immediate priorities being:

- as much time as possible around articulate people
- developing her strengths in active leisure and volunteering
- minimizing her exposure to the things that irritate her about living in the world of disability.

- **Need:** *Marian needs to develop a positive self-image*

Marian does not seem to see herself in a positive light either physically or psychologically and whilst the lifestyle issues mentioned above have an important role to play there are other interventions that will contribute to this area of functioning. Marian does have ideas about preferred hair styles and some types of clothing but she needs more and also needs guidance about some of her choices. There will also be work for those who support Marian in allowing her to experiment within reasonable bounds. It is important to remember also that she may need quite a lot of support in managing some of the self-care skills (for example, hair washing) that may be involved.

Table 7.5: Second of the action implications for Marian

1. Marian should access a therapeutic relationship with someone outside of her general pattern of service provision. Marian has a story to tell and it would help for it to come from her rather than someone like myself. This will be a long-term process and whilst the first priority in finding a therapist should be commitment and enthusiasm it would be preferable, if it can be arranged, for the therapist to be female.

2. From the deep to the not so deep but nonetheless important...Marian should be exposed to visual media such as magazines that offer ideas on style and image. She should also access some regular input from people with more specialist expertise in the 'cosmetic' areas.

3. We should develop a regular (? weekly) system for auditing with Marian how things are going in life. This would involve somebody sitting down with Marian and going over the previous time period, itemizing things that have gone well and things that have gone not so well. This should incorporate visual representation – for example, a picture of weighing scales and writing in the two categories on each side of the scale, also color coding the two categories.

4. We should develop an ongoing life story book with the regular use of photos, cards and other souvenirs to record successful and enjoyable experiences.

5. Although this may seem odd, I think that it is important that we do not criticize Marian for her health concerns. This is a long-term part of who she is, we all know people who are worriers and we need to think how worriers deal with their worries. Whilst we should not actively encourage these things we should always listen as her concerns may have foundations and we need to think about the role of non-prescription pills and potions in the lives of people who are health worriers.

- **Need:** *Marian needs to understand better what is going on in her life and be better able to make real choices, take real control*

I am concerned that the verbal medium is not the easiest one for Marian, despite her apparent proficiency in some areas. The visual channel is historically a strong one for her and also offers automatic compensation for any hidden difficulties such as processing sequence and time lapse, grasping abstractions, short-term memory and focusing attention. One important general guideline: for effective human communication you cannot be too specific and literal and repetition always has a role in getting a message across.

Table 7.6: Third of the action implications for Marian

1. Structure and routine should be seen as a positive and supportive thing for Marian, not a problem.

2. We need to develop a visual medium initially focused on informing Marian about what happens when. I would suggest a weekly timetable for her with key events written in and preferably with some kind of picture or symbol support.

3. Once 2. is developed I would start to engage Marian in adding things to her timetable, choosing from a presented array of options ones that she wants to put into her schedule. This starts us on the long path of Marian taking real control in her life.

- **Need:** *Marian needs to experience a more sustained sense of positive well-being*

All the above needs feed into this central area but there are some additional contributions which have an important role to play. Marian does receive input from the Wellness Team and this will be a key source of guidance on specific things that can be done to promote Marian's physical and emotional well-being. I would also draw attention to the importance of humor and laughter. Marian has a great sense of humor and this is an asset to encourage – this side of her may not be opened up enough. It is a valuable social skill, a general promoter of the feelgood factor and an important way of fracturing mood and distracting when people are ruminating upon the problems that they have.

Table 7.7: Fourth of the action implications for Marian

1. To support Marian's access to the Wellness Team.

2. To look for everyday ways of bringing out Marian's sense of humor and getting her to laugh more often.

- **Need:** *Marian needs to learn better social skills*

Marian has always struggled to really mesh with people and even at the best of times her own behavior has tended to put other people off. Thus in the long run she needs to be more socially skilled if she is to achieve the relationships that are important to her. This cannot be an immediate priority. However, as she recovers her sense of well-being and we all begin to feel comfortable about the lifestyle that we are working towards, more systematic attempts to build social skills will become a priority.

Table 7.8: Fifth of the action implications for Marian

1. We will need to offer Marian specific guidance on the dos and don'ts of specific social situations rather than general social skills training. This advice can be backed with cue cards.

2. We might consider the use of Carol Gray's 'social stories' approach to developing Marian's social understanding and if people are not familiar with this approach I can supply an overview and some materials.

This section has tried to outline some of Marian's longer-term needs insofar as I understand them. There is still much to learn but if the above is on the right lines, working to meet these needs should help Marian to move forward in her life. However, I have no doubt that there will be recurring crises for the time being and consideration needs to be given as to how we help Marian through these periods in the shortest possible time.

Working with Marian when she has lost her overall sense of well-being

There are five elements to this work:

1. Acknowledging to Marian that we are in crisis

    It will be important to ensure that we communicate with Marian that she is unwell and that we now need to work to help her through this phase, rather than pretending that we are carrying on as normal.

2. Following the guidance of the Wellness Team

    Marian is a client of the Wellness Team and their advice will be central in guiding the specific efforts to support Marian in times of crisis.

3. Simplifying life

    Whatever else we do it is likely that in times of crisis we will simplify Marian's life by reducing the demands on her and the number of changes/transitions that she has to cope with. It is vital that we do not abandon all demands, routines and transitions but just that we go down to the bare essentials and then gradually rebuild as she recovers.

4. Supporting the supporters

    Marian will do things that those supporting her find very frustrating. It is important to acknowledge that openly, to have a safe place where people can express their frustrations and work out how best they can deal with the feelings that they have. Otherwise people may take out their frustrations on Marian or give up supporting her, neither of which are constructive outcomes.

5. Managing specific behaviors

    When Marian loses her sense of well-being she will engage more in behaviors that get to other people and an important part of the work will be having clear and agreed plans for responding to incidents. This is not the place for detailing these plans, but in designing plans four key principles will need to be acknowledged:

- *The least restrictive alternative* – our response should be the least restrictive...in the circumstances.

- *The least neglectful alternative* – it is not in Marian's best interests to be left on her own for long periods of time when she is in a crisis phase.

- *The least reinforcing alternative* – all efforts should be made to understand the function(s) of the specific behavior and construct a response that does not actively reinforce the behavior.

- *the alternative least intrusive on the rights of others* – Marian has no right to behave in ways that unreasonably restrict the rights of others (for example, to access communal places).

All these principles will need to be considered and it will rarely be the case that an intervention will satisfy the demands of all these principles. The decision will inevitably be a messy compromise that reflects a considered attempt to act in the way that meets best the requirements of these four perspectives. Sometimes the best decision in the circumstances may be quite an intrusive response, at other times not so.

Concluding remarks

It has been a great privilege to be allowed access to the life of Marian and those who support her. There are many tragic elements to the story so far but Marian is an extraordinary woman with tremendous assets and the potential to lead a fruitful and interesting life. There is still much to learn about the life that will work for her but some of the elements to develop and some of the obstacles to overcome are clear. Whilst I feel very optimistic about her long-term prospects I am cautious about the shorter term and fully expect periods of crisis as we move towards the longer-term goal. This report only has merit insofar as it assists in that longer-term progress and in the shortening of the crisis periods.

The Emperor's Tale

This report is slightly different from the other two. It is not as wide ranging. It is not a specially commissioned report, sought at a time of crisis or reflection. I became involved with Gus as part of a team providing 'wraparound' family support services. These services included weekly family visits from a social worker, behavior consultancy support every two weeks (my role), a certain number of hours of 'inclusion facilitator' time (people to take Gus out into community settings, with a strong leisure/fun element) and a certain number of hours of respite time (managed directly by the parents). In addition there were the more 'routine' services – school, after school and school vacation programs. Gus is an only child, living at home with his parents, both of whom work. It is generally agreed that Gus qualifies for an autism award. The 'wraparound' input began when Gus was 10 years old.

The report was written after working for about a year as part of the wraparound team. It reflects what had been learned through the process of consultation at the time of writing. It was an attempt to draw together some broad understandings of Gus that would guide the more strategic element of our support for him. The more tactical elements were part of his behavior plan, which is summarized in the report. His later plan is included in Chapter 8.

Thinking about Gus

What follows is not an attempt to assess systematically all of Gus's needs. Rather it is a reflection on what the author of this report has learned through the process of getting to know Gus.

Gus is a rather whimsical character. Gus smiles and laughs quite a lot. He is entranced by certain sensory effects (flapping cloth type items, throwing things to the floor) and seems to find the antics of those of us around him quite entertaining. I do not necessarily understand all that he finds amusing but I am delighted that he sees the funny side of the world.

Gus looks upon the social world in a rather puzzled way. Gus finds it hard to understand what people are about – why people do what they do, why he is supposed to do some things and not others, what he is supposed to do in various social situations. He has his own ideas and agenda and finds it hard to grasp that others may have a very different agenda.

Gus has something of an imperial disposition and really should have been born extremely wealthy. He likes and really rather expects people to do things for him rather than do things for himself. He would enjoy having personal servants.

Gus is emotionally expressive. He smiles and laughs, he looks puzzled, he gets excited, he gets upset and sometimes angry. He shows a range of emotions and he shows them strongly. His emotions are both positive and negative, with no particular bias one way or another.

Gus lives more in the sensory world than in the social, material or spiritual world. He loves his flappies, he loves certain kinds of music, he loves certain kinds of touch, he loves his food. But he is also very sensitive — some sounds distress him, he dislikes some touches, he has clear food and music preferences. He can be easily overwhelmed by sensory input and when this happens he becomes very distressed and may hurt whoever is supporting him by grabbing very hard or biting.

There are additional struggles for Gus:

- Gus struggles with the whole area of communicating. He finds it hard to grasp what people want of him and hard to understand information about what is going to happen, what he is going to be doing. He finds it hard to get over to others, in the ways that they prefer to understand things, what it is that he wants — he does not speak or sign though he can use some gestures and can get information from pictures.

- Gus struggles in many areas of learning. Developing most skills takes Gus time.

- Gus struggles to sustain positive health. His bowels are problematic — they can be rather loose, he can get very constipated and he has a lot of gas. He has a history of ear infections, he has sinus problems, he has skin problems (eczema and hives). Whilst these are not continuous problems, they are recurring and need also to be understood in the context of someone who is very sensory focused.

Gus's themes – Gus's behaviors

The aspects of Gus discussed above show clearly in some of the behaviors that give rise to concern.

His sensory focus, his sense of fun and his difficulties in social understanding make it hard for him to inhibit throwing things, grabbing people's glasses, to always be gentle in his physical contacts and to tolerate the intrusion of wearing his own glasses.

His emotional expressiveness, his difficulties in social understanding and his repertoire of skills mean that he can be overwhelmed in some situations and not have the skills either to deal with it himself or seek help from others. He may then lose control and do things that hurt others and that effectively remove him from sources of discomfort.

His struggles in learning and his imperial disposition mean that some important skills have not yet been mastered – communication and toilet training are two important areas of concern at the present time.

Gus's health issues and his sensory focus contribute to the occasional use of mild forms of self-injury and more generally reduced tolerance, likely to be implicated in tantrums and aggression.

This not to suggest that such a 'thematic analysis' is a full account of all the behaviors. For such an account, additional functional assessment of specific behaviors may contribute further insights. However, the themes do point to some of Gus's longer-term needs that should inform the kinds of support that Gus receives.

From themes and behaviors to needs

Gus will need help to structure his time and to discriminate what he can use for his sensory hobbies and what not. He will need proactive support so that unstructured time is reduced and clear signals (for example, hobby boxes, back packs) to indicate where favored items are kept that he can help himself to.

Gus needs sustained work to build his communication skills – both understanding and expression. At present, pictures or icons seem the easiest medium to work in, alongside speech; but Gus is beginning to imitate movements, so signs could also be considered as part of a total communication approach.

Gus needs to acquire the concept of gentle touch so that he can be more helpful in how he handles himself and other people.

Gus needs help to maximize his sense of personal well-being. His physicians will of course deal with specific medical concerns. However, on a more general everyday basis, diet and exercise can make a very positive contribution. The family has been considering the trial of a gluten/casein free diet. Exercise, especially if regular and aerobic, could help to build Gus's general health and also reduce the likelihood of him becoming overwhelmed emotionally in some situations.

Gus needs sustained help to build his tolerance of ordinary situations that he finds uncomfortable. He has evidenced clearly that he can habituate to things (for example, the sound of a blender) given time and repeated, gradual exposure. It is important to open Gus to as many opportunities as possible so that in the long term he can make real choices about what he does and does not want to do.

Combining exposure with communication, Gus's sensitivities need to be understood, the early warning signs identified and a communication plan put in place so that he can ask to leave a situation.

Gus is now of an age where toileting becomes a very significant issue socially. This will require sustained work in all environments, initially targeting urination in the toilet (bowel issues may require separate consideration as Gus evidences more concern in this area).

Concluding remarks

Gus has made significant progress in all areas of immediate concern. There is still much to be done – to understand in detail his needs, to develop his skills, to provide appropriate environmental adaptations and to ensure that the family as a whole can experience a reasonable quality of life. The journey is a long one.

Table 7.9: Summary of behavior consultancy work (to the time of writing the report)		
BEHAVIORS OF CONCERN	**CONSULTANCY INPUTS**	**CURRENT STATUS OF BEHAVIOR**
Throwing things	• Keep readily accessible self-occupying materials • Redirect to materials as he becomes excited • Remove, for a period of time, items targeted for more ritualistic throwing • Get Gus to pick up solid objects thrown	Reduced to much lower level though still occurs
Incontinence	• Schedule some regular toileting occasions, using visual communication system • Materially reinforce proximity to toilet for increasing durations • Use a stimulus for urination (bathtime, taps running) and redirect aim! • Direct to toilet or bucket when diaper taken off spontaneously • Provide portaloo in bedroom for bowel movements	• Will cooperate with toileting prompts and stay for a reasonable time • A few successes at urinating in the toilet • No progress on bowel training

Aggressive behaviors (bite, pinch, pull hair)	• Use visual communication to convey information and encourage choice making • Distract if build up of agitation • Firm directions to move to a quiet/non-crowded area if agitation continues • General work on notion of 'gentle touch'	These behaviors are now rare. Most recent instances have involved unfamiliar and very stimulating situations that have got too much for Gus
Self-injury (face slapping, self-biting, head banging)	No specific additional program suggested (elements of the work on aggression are of course relevant)	Self-biting and head banging have been very rare. Face slapping fluctuates over time. It tends to come in phases and is at present the focus of more detailed assessment work
Tantrums (jumping up and down, making a lot of noise, sometimes accompanied by face slapping)	No specific additional program suggested (elements of the work on aggression are of course relevant)	Tantrums fluctuate over time and are at present the focus of more detailed assessment work
Grabbing other people's glasses	Not been the focus of specific concern	
Wearing own glasses	Encouraged at meal times	Little progress and not clear what benefit Gus himself experiences from wearing them

Update to time of writing the book

I continue to be part of the wraparound team – and it is truly a team in this case. Huge progress has been made – there is still much to be done. Gus overall is a happier guy. Behaviors do fluctuate over time (we have identified December–January as a time when there is a recurring 'spike') but there has been very marked and sustained improvement in the aggression, self-injury and tantrums overall. Throwing objects comes and goes but is currently much reduced. Visual communication is now much more a part of every environment. We continue to encourage vocal and motor imitation and Gus now has a number of gestures and at least one sign with communicative purposes. He has grasped 'gentle touch'. Gus has been to many more community based activities…and enjoyed them, including the movies. He has built his tolerance of hair washing, tooth brushing, having his hair cut (though still a major operation) and dental examination. He is managing more basic self-care skills for himself. He has coped with his first overnight stays away from home. There has been no progress on toileting but this is now the focus of a major effort in all environments (Gus makes progress insofar as we really focus in on an area and the reality is that such a focus is usually only possible for one area at a time). His gastrointestinal functioning is improved although an underlying problem has not been diagnosed. As well as the specific changes we are also seeing a more general attentiveness to things social – it is easier to get Gus's attention and cooperation and he initiates social contact a lot more. To achieve all this requires close and sustained support – Gus is critically dependent on the support we give him; changes are not self-generated. Hence the need for team support to a family – without this, no individual or family could sustain the energy required. If people burn out, Gus's progress halts. Understanding this dynamic is a key to designing services that support all members of a family and that give a quality of life for all.

Concluding remarks to the chapter

It is hoped that the above reports illustrate how a large volume of information can be sifted and then woven into a plausible story with practical implications. They tend to focus more on broad themes that illuminate why particular behaviors occur. There is some consideration of immediate determinants of incidents but this element is probably more obviously demonstrated in the behavior plans included in Chapter 8.

CHAPTER 8

Organizing the Practice

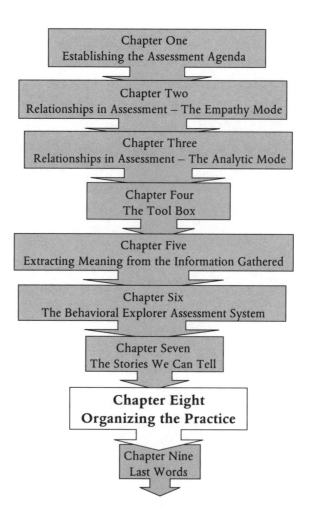

Chapter One
Establishing the Assessment Agenda

Chapter Two
Relationships in Assessment – The Empathy Mode

Chapter Three
Relationships in Assessment – The Analytic Mode

Chapter Four
The Tool Box

Chapter Five
Extracting Meaning from the Information Gathered

Chapter Six
The Behavioral Explorer Assessment System

Chapter Seven
The Stories We Can Tell

**Chapter Eight
Organizing the Practice**

Chapter Nine
Last Words

Many people with developmental disabilities act in ways that give rise to concern and prompt us to ask 'Why does she do that?' It would not be desirable for all these people to be publicly identified as problematic and to be the focus of a major, public effort at assessment and planned intervention (see Chapter 1). It would be better if some of these issues were resolved more informally in the course of day-to-day support. For those people who might benefit from some kind of public acknowledgement of their behavior a comprehensive assessment may not always be necessary – the problem and its solution may be relatively straightforward. Even if, in principle, a comprehensive assessment was to be regarded as desirable in every case, in practice there are not and never will be the resources necessary to do this.

Thus on grounds of desirability, necessity and feasibility it seems important to think about conceptualizing practice as operating at a number of levels; and that you only move to another level if a problem has not been resolved by working at the previous level. In this chapter we will think in terms of three levels – that is an arbitrary number; there is no claim that there are only three levels or that this is somehow the 'best' way of conceptualizing practice. It is illustrative and part of the struggle to ensure that as many people as possible receive competent support in their everyday lives around those issues that we designate 'behavioral'.

Level 1 – Mindful/reflective practice…paperless support!

At this level all the work is done internally within the individuals who support a person with developmental disabilities and by discussion between them. What is required is that those supporting the individual have an internal framework for understanding people, one that recognizes multiple contributors and different time frames; and that people be prepared to ask questions of themselves and between themselves. It requires that the supporter(s) mentally step back from the concern…hit the pause button and stop reacting reflexively. It requires a focus on information and may require inhibiting opinion so that the mind is open to new perspectives. Key questions are summarized in Table 8.1.

Table 8.1: Questions to assist mindful/reflective practice around behavioral concerns

- What is the 'problem' – what exactly is the person doing that makes me concerned?

- Is this really a problem...and if so, whose problem is it?

- What do I know of this person – especially strong preferences and the important issues in life from his point of view?

- What do I know of the situations when the behavior is most and least likely to occur?

- When the person does this, what do I think it means?

- What do I envisage the person doing in the situations when the behavior occurs if he did not do the behavior of concern – what would he do instead?

- Have I worked successfully through anything like this before – with this individual or any other? If so, what did I do?

- Has this issue been addressed successfully for this individual before? If so, how was it done?

At some point in the process of reflection, time needs to be allocated to trying to get close to the reality of the other person, to get a sense of how it is for the other making his way though the world.

Out of this period of questioning and reflection come ideas of things that we will try to work on consistently to see if a difference can be made (judged informally). There is one further reflective check:

If my behavior was of concern to others how would I feel about being supported in the ways that I am planning to support this individual?

It would be nice to think that reflective practice so defined is obvious and done by everyone automatically. Unfortunately that is far from the truth. Behaviors generate strong feelings and strong opinions. Supporters often cast themselves in the roles with which they feel familiar, especially 'parent' to 'child', and react as they would to their own children or as they were reacted to as children. Disabilityland tends to be an isolated place and is notorious for developing bizarre norms as to how problems should be reacted to ('Ignore bad behavior', 'Don't show your feelings', 'Always squeal "good job" in a high-pitched voice whenever anyone does anything regarded as vaguely appropriate'). And it is human nature when faced with an unpleasant problem to offload it onto someone else. It is especially good to blame someone else ('It's because the parents spoil her') because you can then combine feelings of moral self-righteousness with the relief of not having to do anything.

Reflective practice is not really common sense and therefore not very common. It is unlikely to occur by chance. It needs cultivating and the prime vehicle for its cultivation is through ongoing mechanisms of staff support. Those who are working on a day-to-day basis with people who have developmental disabilities need space and time to step back from their everyday duties and the support of someone who will guide them through the process of reflecting on practice. Such support should really come through the line of management although agencies may contract this role to an outsider. By participating in such support mechanisms it becomes possible to internalize the sort of questioning envisaged earlier in this section. In the context of such ongoing support mechanisms training can play a useful role in further developing staff's capacities for insight, understanding and practical support strategies. In the absence of such ongoing support mechanisms, training is mostly a waste of time.

One would think that human service agencies would readily embrace such systems of support. Some do; many do not. Even if an agency acknowledges the need at some level, the most common response is to try to deal with it by throwing training at people. Yet the development of good reflective practice will lead to the informal resolution of many behavioral issues. The price of failure at this level is for many more people to be publicly identified as challenging, the unnecessary loss of many staff who get burned out around behaviors, a vast increase in paperwork and bureaucratic involvement and an ever increasing demand for access to expensive experts who will 'fix' the problem. This outcome is disastrous for everyone, except the bureaucrats and 'experts'! The conclusions one draws from this will depend upon one's propensity for conspiracy theorizing.

Thus developing good reflective practice should be a priority for any agency involved in supporting people with developmental disabilities, particularly if the agency likes to embrace those whose behavior gives rise to concern. However, reflective practice is not a cure-all. Some problems will not yield to good practice at this level and there is a need to move to a more formal level.

Level 2 – Intermediate level assessment and planning

At the second level we move to a formal acknowledgement that there are behavioral concerns that do not seem to be yielding to current (we hope, reflective) practice. Formal acknowledgement means that we communicate with all those who support the person who is of concern, that we take steps to gather, record and summarize assessment information and that from this we write up a plan that details how we will work with the individual in order to effect specific changes in behavior and well-being.

The content of assessment at this level will include both general information about the person and specific information about the behaviors of concern, with a focus on immediate and short-term influences (see Table 8.2 for details).

Once the information is assembled it will need to be summarized and a plan written detailing the specific supports that will be offered (guidelines for plan writing are included later in the chapter).

It is both feasible and desirable that all services offering support to people with developmental disabilities aspire to competence at this level as well as level 1. Services will of course need to consider their overall resourcing to enable this to happen, principally to create the time for those involved on a day-to-day basis to carry out these activities. There are some training issues but these are fairly minimal at this level. Although behavioral 'experts' (psychologists, psychiatrists, behavior analysts) often become involved at this stage that may not be necessary or even desirable. Such experts should really be reserved for the hard questions, and only the hard questions.

Table 8.2: Core assessment areas for Level 2 behavioral work

- An overview of the person's preferences (likes and dislikes).

- An overview of the person's competences (knowledge and skills – present, emergent and absent).

- A summary of recent life events (last two years).

- A physical health check.

- Recording of incidents of the behavior(s) of concern.

- Completion of the three questions exercise.

- A system for monitoring behavior (recording and graphing frequency/duration).

As one such expert I am in some ways very happy when people ask me a question to which the answer is 'Let's try keeping some detailed records of specific incidents'. Very happy, because it's easy money; but very sad, because resources are being burned up by involving me at this level, resources better devoted to practical assistance to the individual and those who support her.

Work at this level will yield to improvement in many behavioral concerns. If it is planned and carried out by those involved on a day-to-day basis this can yield a growth in confidence and self-esteem for all and a strengthening of the sense of 'team' – the progress can be clearly attributed to the group's work together. However, not all behavioral issues will be resolved by work at this level. For some there will be a need for a more comprehensive assessment, which we will designate as our level 3.

Level 3 – Comprehensive assessment

The major additional information needs for level 3 work are summarized in Table 8.3.

Table 8.3: Level 3 information needs

- At this level we will need all the information from level 2 plus the additional areas detailed in this book. We will need more detailed personal information, particularly around personality, emotional functioning and social understanding.

- We will need a more detailed life history.

- We may include more detailed assessment of immediate and short-term influences, through analog sessions or use of a computer assisted observational system.

- We will need information about some of the longer-term factors – social systemic issues, quality of life issues, physical and mental health issues.

- We will need a clearer image of the 'ideal' life that would work well for the individual and the non-negotiable elements of that life.

This level of assessment may well involve access to specialists of one kind or another. It may also involve additional resourcing of the observational component so that information can be gathered by someone whose only job is to do that, someone who is not a participant in the everyday work of support – likewise, resourcing for a more detailed lifestyle analysis.

Summarizing the outcome of assessment at this level follows the same principles and guidelines that we use at level 2. It is likely to be a harder job and to take more time. It is not a job that should be automatically allocated to any one professional group – there is nothing to suggest that only psychologists/psychiatrists can do this. It is important that it be clear, in the context of the particular individual and his supporters, who is pulling together the various inputs and weaving them into a coherent plan of action. This point was stressed earlier in the book but is considered further here. Without this role being clearly designated, the outcome of a comprehensive assessment can be very negative. Lots of inputs are received. High status 'experts' become involved. The ownership of those who are involved on a day-to-day basis is undermined as each expert asserts what needs to be done and, overtly or by implication, criticizes what has been done before. The views of the experts may be in conflict or hard to reconcile and each expert will usually assert the primacy of his own perspective. In these circumstances, the move to a comprehensive assessment can have very negative consequences for the individual – those supporting on a day-to-day basis become uncertain, undermined or conflicted and from there it is only a short step to a *de facto* collapse of the social support system (usually disguised in professional speak as 'needing to move to a more specialized placement').

Thus managing the process becomes a key issue as we shift to level 3. This probably merits a chapter in its own right but for now it is important to stress that it needs to be made clear who it is that will maintain the coordination of the support to the individual once the cavalry has been summoned. A key role at this level is to maintain the sense of ownership of the issues by those people who are currently supporting the individual.

As for level 2, level 3 will involve a written plan detailing the support work to be provided on a day-to-day basis. Much of the content will be similar to that involved at level 2 although there may be more interventions, more detailed interventions and additional inputs that are not part of everyday social support (for example, access to therapy). It therefore seems appropriate at this point to consider what needs to go into written plans about behavior.

Behavior plans – paper and practice

There are a number of reasons why those who present to us significant behavioral challenges will acquire the written documents often referred to as 'behavior plans'. These reasons include:

1.   The need to 'contractualize' support arrangements. As already discussed (Chapter 1) it is in no one's real interest to be designated publicly as behaviorally problematic/socially deviant. There are costs to the individual in terms of public reputation. We also know that people so designated are vulnerable to abusive practices of many kinds. It is therefore

important to spell out the steps that we are taking to offset these costs and to produce the benefits that are desired.

> *If I am going to declare your behavior problematic I solemnly undertake to do things that will make life better for all of us.*

A behavior plan is a contract between the individual and those who support her – that if we are going to bring these (behavioral) matters to the forefront we are also promising to do something constructive to resolve the problems. What we are promising is to offer the support spelled out in the plan. In this way a behavior plan should be seen as establishing an entitlement for the individual – an entitlement to receive the support spelled out in the plan.

2. The need to sustain and improve the quality of support. Following from the above, a written plan makes it easier to be clear about what we are doing. It makes it easier to establish consistency across those who support the person and to introduce new staff to the ways in which we work for the person. A written plan does not guarantee these outcomes – just because something is on paper does not mean that it is used. These outcomes are only achieved insofar as the document is used during day-to-day problem solving, is used to induct new staff and is actively monitored for implementation. However, in the context of these activities, a written plan can be very helpful in sustaining constructive work across different people and over time.

3. The development of a learning bank. By detailing plans and monitoring their effectiveness it becomes possible to develop a learning bank, a repository of supports that have and have not been helpful. This can be an individual bank, to be drawn on just by the particular person and those who support her. An organization might think to establish a more general bank detailing helpful and unhelpful practices that might be drawn upon to assist individuals who access the service in the future or who get into difficulties in the future. To my knowledge this use of written plans has not been

systematically exploited. There is often 'folklore' around individuals and those who work in the field for a long period of time developing an internal bank of ideas to draw upon. However, there does seem merit in exploiting experience more systematically, and written plans plus the monitoring that should go with them open up this possibility, especially given the new technologies for database management.

4.   Satisfying the needs of bureaucrats. People who present significant behavioral challenges may well attract additional resourcing. In most countries this will mean allocation of additional monies from that part of the public purse designated for people with developmental disabilities. Those who disburse public funds can and should demand accountability for their use. The most popular form of accountability is paperwork accountability – something is put on paper that indicates the use to which funds have been put and presumably justifies that usage. Here is not the place to argue whether such paper trails are either necessary or sufficient for real accountability. The reality is that many service providers will be required to generate some kind of paperwork around what they are doing to address the issues raised by people whose behavior is cause for concern and who have been allocated additional resources on this basis.

Thus for a number of reasons there is a need for documentation around behavioral issues. Whilst the need is clear, the standards that such documentation must meet are not always so clear. In some places there may be standards enshrined in law; in most places there are not. There is not even any real professional consensus on what constitutes a 'good' behavior plan. Thus the present ideas are put forward to help those who are trying to construct useful documentation in a vacuum of guidance as to the standards such documentation should meet. There is no guarantee that the recommendations here will meet specific local standards but in the absence of these it at least provides a starting point.

What a plan needs to show — core elements

Agencies will vary in the terminology preferred and the design/layout of their paperwork. Whatever the preferences in this respect, a written plan should always contain the core elements described in Table 8.4.

Table 8.4 Core elements of a behavior plan

- **A specific definition of the behavior(s) that the plan will address**: the concern should be spelled out in terms of observable behaviors. The statement should be specific enough so that anyone would know whether or not the behavior occurred.

- **Current level(s) of the defined behaviors**: a baseline in terms of the frequency/duration of the behaviors as measured over a period of weeks or months.

- **A justification for intervention**: there need to be good reasons that justify people organizing themselves to follow a plan intended to change the behavior of the person in question. These need to be spelled out and it should also be clear who is giving consent to what is going to be done.

- **A description of what has been done to try to make sense of the behavior(s)**: this will spell out the assessment work that has been carried out.

- **A summary of what factors are thought to be contributing to the behavior(s)**: this details the 'working theory' that has been derived from the assessment and that will inform the plan to be followed.

- **The plan**: this should lay out in clear, accessible everyday language the things that will be done to support the individual that it is hoped will lead to behavior change. The standard here is that any new member of staff should be able to read/listen to this and know what is to be done.

- **Monitoring**: this section describes how behavior will be tracked and the effectiveness of the plan monitored.

- **Outcomes targeted**: specific targets should be set to indicate what change is expected over what period of time if the plan is implemented and is effective.

Developing plans

Plans can be developed in a number of ways. One common model is to ask an 'expert' to assess the problem and write the plan, rather in the way a doctor writes a prescription. The role of those who work on a day-to-day basis with the individual is to give information to the expert and then follow the plan laid down.

This model is appealing. It is plausible. In the author's experience it is largely ineffective except in highly authoritarian environments with strong coercive controls; and these are not, by definition, the kinds of environments in which people with disabilities are going to be able to get on with their lives (unless of course they have signed up voluntarily for the armed forces or for a certain kind of religious order). It is more effective if those who are to implement a plan are closely involved in its development and establish some sense of ownership of the plan. Even if an 'expert' is involved such an expert is more likely to be effective if she works in a collaborative way, which recognizes that everyone has something to contribute. The collaboration needs to be ongoing. The initial plan is drawn up together, worked on together, monitored and reviewed together, amended together. It is a team effort. The expert is more in the role of coach or, to use our earlier imagery, a guide for a particular terrain that is being crossed on the journey.

Some working plans

To bring this issue of written plans to some kind of life, we include here current plans for two of the people whose assessments are included in Chapter 7. Once again, these are not put forward as perfect documents and the temptation to make them look better has been resisted – these are the documents in the hands of the people currently supporting Jack and Gus. They will illustrate some of the difficulties that arise in the real world (for example, in gathering monitoring data). They are included to assist those who are coming new to writing behavior plans and who might find models more helpful than a list of instructions.

Jack's plan

This plan focuses on one specific behavior. This plan was developed as a follow on from the assessment although there was a considerable time gap, as the behavior did not occur for a long period of time. It is currently in operation.

BEHAVIOR SUPPORT CONTRACT
between Mr JACK LAD and BEACON SERVICES

This contract was drawn up **March 2001**

Mr Lad receives Regional Center CPC services from **Ms Sarah Wainwright**

NOTE: THIS CONTRACT MUST BE READ ALONGSIDE BEACON DOCUMENT **'JACK'S SUPPORT PLAN'**

Behaviors of concern

Types

1. *Aggression* – hits, kicks, bites others…or attempts to.

Jack does behave in other ways that give rise to concern but these are not the focus of the present contract.

Frequency

The detailed daily notes kept by Beacon have not been fully analyzed but on the basis of the recently introduced system of incident recording:

Aggression – once a day …March 9th to 12th, 2001

Justification for intervention

The behavior does violate the rights of others to be safe at work and breaks the law of the land. It also costs Jack a lot in social support. Jack has the capacity to charm other people and draw them into his circle of support in a way that enriches his life. However, when he hurts those who support him they often lose their confidence around him and sooner or later they withdraw from his circle. The behavior, as well as other behaviors that he exhibits, has resulted in Jack receiving long-term, powerful psychotropic medications and this too has costs for him. Thus the behavior in question is very costly for Jack and others and it would seem justifiable to take planned steps to try to reduce the likelihood of such incidents occurring.

Our understanding of these behaviors (functional assessment)

Information gathering

John Clements completed an earlier, detailed assessment of the kinds of issues that are reflected in Jack's behaviors. There has also been ongoing consultation work between Beacon and John Clements, a review of the daily notes kept by Beacon, detailed recording of recent incidents and time spent by John Clements interacting with and observing Jack at home. There have been many meetings of all those involved in supporting Jack which have helped to develop the understanding of what the aggression is about.

Contributory factors identified

Immediate influences: Immediate antecedents include Jack being offered something that he does not want or there being some kind of a limit set on what he does. Jack is often in a highly aroused state at these times and sometimes the onset of such a state occurs without clear environmental triggers. Thus the antecedents for some incidents are high arousal marked by intense body movements and somebody being within easy reach. In some cases the behavior may have maintaining consequences – people may withdraw their suggestions and move out of Jack's space. There is also some evidence that the response of the target person has some influence – Jack may be more likely to target those who react in an anxious or uncertain way. However, it is also likely that some incidents are not maintained by consequences but are part of a more general overarousal and loss of behavioral control/inhibition.

Ecological/setting conditions: The mid afternoon (around 3 pm) is a higher risk time. Likewise if Jack is in general in a highly agitated or aroused state.

Other contributors: Jack loves to be in control and tends not to be too tolerant of dissent. He has engaged in these behaviors long term.

However, Jack also has a range of significant physical health issues that impact upon his well-being and stress him greatly. He has experienced much trauma in his life and he has a good memory. Whilst Jack has communication skills adequate for his basic needs he does not have the skills to pinpoint what is troubling him and to negotiate his way in problem situations. Jack also seems to 'run' some kind of internal 'movies' and 'dialogues' and these can sometimes generate strong surges of negative feelings.

Medications
Major and minor tranquilizers

And therefore the support contract is
The things that we will do to prevent the negative behaviors and to promote positive functioning, personal satisfaction and well-being:

- ✓ We are organizing a review of Jack's physical health.

- ✓ We will work hard to ensure full and clear communication between those who support Jack in the day and those who support him at home.

- ✓ Jack functions better with a routine although he often likes to have different routines with different people.

- ✓ At this time we will 'stay close' to Jack. We will hang out where we can see him (as long as he tolerates this) so that we can observe changes and also reduce the effort required if Jack has something to communicate with us. We will continue to respond to all reasonable requests from Jack including 'tickle'. We will try to sit at or below his level and talk relatively quietly. The 'close' here is psychological – if Jack is becoming very agitated, we should be out of immediate striking range.

- ✓ If Jack has withdrawn to his bedroom we will try to 'stay close' to him by dropping in and interacting with him for brief periods (little and often may work better than extended periods unless Jack clearly requests that we stay).

✓ We will keep an ongoing stock of novelty items and relevant pictures and as part of 'staying close' will try to distract him with these. We will also 'drop hints' with words and pictures of activities that are potentially available (park, store, garden-bugs). Getting Jack to take enjoyable walks round the garden or park in the late afternoon would likely help his mood.

✓ We will try to make mid afternoon as pleasurable as possible – for example, favorite drinks/snacks on the table, seeding the air with interesting aromas, running a bath to see if he would like to take a bath in the afternoon as well as the morning.

✓ When Jack speaks he is sometimes asking for things but sometimes he is starting a conversation – 'Tommy' may be a discussion about remembering the people who have worked with him; 'Grandma's house' may be a conversation about that house and what he saw there or about other houses he has visited. We will try to expand on such conversations. We will know pretty quickly if we have got it wrong and Jack is asking for the thing he has just said – I think it unlikely that 'Pizza' is an opener for an extended discussion on great pizzas I have eaten or the relative merits of Round Table versus Pizza Hut!

✓ We will only take Jack out in a car where he can sit in the back, on the opposite side to the driver.

✓ If we observe Jack becoming very intensely engaged in his internal world (staring hard at his hand, mouthing intensely, intense spasms running through his body), we will try to break this up by asking him what he sees/hears, asking if he 'hurts'.

✓ If we have any reason to believe that Jack is in pain we will encourage him to take a painkiller (in line with the advice that we receive from Dr Smith).

✓ If Jack is moving around the house in a very agitated fashion we will try to position ourselves so that we can see him without following him around. We will intervene as little as is compatible with his safety and talk quietly to reassure him.

The ways that we will respond when the behaviors occur

- If Jack hits/kicks or tries to bite we will block or move out of range whilst at the same time switching our personal style with him. We will take a very assertive line, standing up, holding our ground and telling him firmly that 'That is not so sweet and you need to back off', indicating where he can go (for example, 'You need to take some quiet time in the front room or your bedroom').

- If he continues to aggress, 'Jack's Support Plan' does authorize moving behind him, holding his clothes and directing him away. The training currently being organized may give us other options for responding.

- If he still comes after us we can either repeat the above or tell him, again very assertively, that we do not want to be around him when he is like this and we are going to take some quiet time for ourselves, removing ourselves then to a room where we can close the door on him.

- If the situation continues and there is no sign of regaining control, we will contact the 'on call' person for extra support.

- Only if the situation is continuing out of control after going through the above options should 911 be called (we will be prepping the local police about Jack and the situations that can arise).

We will monitor this plan by

1. *Recording* on the incident forms all occurrences of aggression/attempted aggression.
2. *Maintaining* the detailed daily logs.
3. *Regular consultation* with Beacon's behavior consultant and other team members.

It is our hope that we will achieve the following outcomes

By September 2001

Aggression to 0 times a month for 3 consecutive months.

Gus's plan

This is not Gus's first plan but it is the one current at the time of writing.

Behaviors of concern

Types

1. *Hurt others* – pinch, scratch, pull hair, bite

2. *Push others*

3. *Hurt self* – slap face, bang head, bite self

4. *Property damage* – throwing objects, tipping lamps

5. *Intrusive noise* – vocalizing at high pitch/intensity.

Frequency

Frequency and intensity fluctuate over time and detailed monitoring systems are not in place. General monitoring is carried out through the regular consultation process.

Justification for intervention

Mr and Mrs Jones chose these behaviors as important to reduce. Hurting others does violate their rights to be safe. Our general duty of care requires that we act to reduce self-harm. Property damage impacts unreasonably on the quality of the home environment and involves the family in additional expenditures. The intrusive noise can be unpleasant for others and does raise the likelihood of Gus having a negative reputation – thus, it has led to complaints and disparaging remarks from the neighbors.

Our understanding of these behaviors (functional assessment)

Information gathering

Assessment has been undertaken through the regular process of consultation that was begun in February 99. A detailed report on

Gus's needs was completed in February 2000. Access was given to the school based functional assessment and behavior plan. There have also been some time periods when more detailed recordings of incidents have been made.

Contributory factors identified

HURTING OTHERS/SELF

The **hurting others** and **hurting self** are seen as part of the same response class.

Immediate influences: Immediate antecedents are Gus being denied something that he has requested (especially food) or being directed to move on from a situation. It is also likely that there are internal antecedents such as physical discomfort. Whilst Gus copes successfully with most denials and directions, a key antecedent factor is his overall level of arousal – high arousal is usually part of the triggering complex. Consequences are the relief of discomfort and it may be also that sometimes food arrives close in time to an outburst.

Ecological/setting conditions: Incidents are much more likely when Gus is unwell – constipation, sinus problems, skin problems. Incidents are much more likely in unfamiliar but highly stimulating environments.

Other contributors: Gus experiences a very significant difficulty in communicating his wants and needs. He has difficulty in monitoring his internal states and lacks coping skills for dealing with his discomforts. He has a number of recurring health difficulties.

PUSHING OTHERS

Immediate influences: Immediate antecedents are Gus not wanting to do something and consequences are that sometimes requests are withdrawn.

Ecological/setting conditions: Not clear at this time.

Other contributors: Gus experiences a very significant difficulty in communicating his wants and needs.

PROPERTY DAMAGE

Immediate influences: Immediate antecedents are Gus not being involved in a structured task, especially if he is also walking around (incidents are less likely when he is seated). The consequences are the sensory stimulation achieved which includes 'exciting' social responses from others.

Ecological/setting conditions: Incidents occur mainly in the home and at unstructured times.

Other contributors: Gus experiences a very significant difficulty in communicating his wants and needs. He also has a long-term interest in certain kinds of sensory stimulation. He is also very limited in his ability to occupy himself for extended periods and is, at the time of writing, generally rather restless.

INTRUSIVE NOISE

Immediate influences: Immediate antecedents are Gus being involved in something that he really hates (for example, hair washing) or him not being involved in a structured task. It is not clear that there are maintaining consequences – the behaviors may just be part of an 'upset state'. It is possible that sometimes the behavior is a form of self-stimulation.

Ecological/setting conditions: Incidents are more likely if Gus is in discomfort – physical or emotional.

Other contributors: Gus experiences a very significant difficulty in communicating his wants and needs. He has long-term health problems with his bowels and skin. He is also very sensitive to 'intrusions' around his head and face.

And therefore the support plan is

The things that we will do to prevent the negative behaviors and to promote positive functioning and well-being:

- ✓ We will continue to develop Gus's picture based communication system, both to explain to him what activities are coming up and to get him to express his choices/preferences. We will also use this as part of the hair washing and hair cutting routines.

- ✓ We will expand Gus's range of life experiences so that he gets used to more situations and is not so easily overwhelmed by them.

- ✓ We will monitor Gus's health and intervene early (for example, to keep his bowels working, to alleviate skin discomfort).

✓ When introducing Gus to new and very stimulating situations, we will try to start off with spending only short times in them and gradually building up. We are using this graded approach with both the hair washing and the hair cutting.

✓ We will try to involve Gus in as much physical exercise as possible.

✓ When Gus touches us lightly we will always respond with attention and a check to see if there is anything that he wants.

✓ If Gus is starting to escalate the intensity of tapping us we will remind him to be 'gentle' and accompany this with a light stroke of his arm.

✓ If Gus is exercising a choice and saying 'No' we will not allow him to push us but will encourage a sweeping hand gesture instead.

✓ When walking downstairs with Gus we will try not to be in front of him, with our back to him.

✓ When leaving a much-enjoyed situation we will try to ensure that we have attractive 'transition activities' so that Gus's attention is focused onto something positive.

✓ We will develop 'hobby boxes' for Gus in which we put light objects that are of interest to him and have a house rule that he can only play with the objects in his boxes. We will change the objects frequently.

✓ We will lock away certain areas of the home (for example, the cupboards in Mr and Mrs's Jones room) and carpet a floor area that is a favorite 'target zone' for throwing.

✓ We will involve Gus more routinely in helping out with chores around the home.

✓ We will have a house rule that Gus cannot walk round the house holding anything other than his 'flappies' – he must sit down with cups, plates and any heavy toys.

The ways that we will respond when the behaviors occur

• If Gus is hurting us/others we will speak firmly (but not loudly) to him – we will direct him to put his hands down and/or move away. We will at the same time physically break his grip and block with our hands further attempts at hurting.

- If Gus is biting himself or slapping his face we will try to soothe him and offer him our hands to hold or offer him his flappies but otherwise not physically intervene. If he is banging his head against a solid surface we will place a 'cushioning' item between his head and the surface and verbally encourage him to calm down but not directly physically intervene.

- If Gus becomes very, very aroused but is not hurting himself or others we will give him space and time to calm down but not otherwise intervene. As his level of arousal decreases we will offer activities to try to help him refocus.

- If Gus is starting to slap at furnishings, threatening to throw or tip lamps, we will check to see if he is 'teasing' – if so, we will ignore. However, if he is not 'teasing' we will firmly direct him to put his hands down and quickly move to prompt his cooperation. We will then redirect him to his 'hobby boxes' or some other activity.

- If Gus has already thrown or tipped we may direct him to his room whilst we tidy up and calm ourselves down. Alternatively we may withhold positive interaction with him for a period of time following the incident. The time periods here should be in the 5–10 minute frame.

We will monitor this plan by

The ongoing process of consultation with the family.

It is our hope that we will achieve the following outcomes

By September 2001

Hurt others to 0 times a month for 3 consecutive months.
Push others to 0 times a month for 3 consecutive months.
Hurt self to 0 times a month for 3 consecutive months.
No more than one incident of property damage a week in the previous month.
No complaints from the neighbors for 3 consecutive months.

Concluding remarks

There is much still to learn about how to effect changes in human behavior in non-toxic ways. Psychology is in its infancy as a science. However, a lot has been learned about effective ways of supporting people that do lead to the reduction in socially costly behaviors. What has proved difficult is to get these support practices into widespread use so that the people with developmental disabilities who do present us with significant challenges receive the most competent support possible. There are many reasons for this gap between what is known and what is done. It is hoped that the present chapter makes a small contribution to the narrowing of that gap.

CHAPTER 9

Last Words

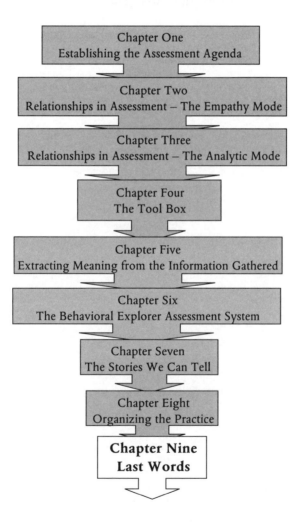

Chapter One
Establishing the Assessment Agenda

Chapter Two
Relationships in Assessment – The Empathy Mode

Chapter Three
Relationships in Assessment – The Analytic Mode

Chapter Four
The Tool Box

Chapter Five
Extracting Meaning from the Information Gathered

Chapter Six
The Behavioral Explorer Assessment System

Chapter Seven
The Stories We Can Tell

Chapter Eight
Organizing the Practice

Chapter Nine
Last Words

So, we come to the end of our 'travel guide'. It is hoped that it is a practical guide. However, underpinning the text are a number of core beliefs, beliefs that are personal to the author and which rise to the surface every so often. These include:

- The belief that strong human relationships are central to what we do. These relationships need to be based upon respect and value. Achieving such relationships with those people whom society designates as 'developmentally disabled' is difficult and requires an ongoing personal struggle.

- The belief that everyday life is the key to the most significant changes in human well-being and behavior. It is the relationships and activities, the patterns and the rhythms, the things little and large that go on day in, day out that make the difference. The 'exotic' interventions that we identify as 'therapies' may, in some cases, exert some small influence but it is as nothing compared with the role of everyday life. This means that those people who participate in an individual's everyday life are the key to efforts at change.

- The belief that the domains on knowledge we designate as 'psychological' are useful but they are not rocket science. What we know of the reasons why people do what they do and what we can do to assist a fellow human being move on; these areas of knowledge can be made accessible to all. It is a major role for those who have been lucky enough to be trained academically in these areas to ensure such accessibility and to put whatever knowledge and skills have been gained in the hands of those who can make best use of them, those who participate in the everyday lives of individuals in distress.

- The belief that change in behavioral and emotional functioning is effected by things done repeatedly, things done day in, day out; that change tends to take place in small steps, accumulating over time; that the trajectory of change is fluctuating, not smooth.

- The belief that science and values are complementary, not opposed. Science is a vehicle for listening and learning, for getting closer to 'what is' and for opening the mind, for challenging personal prejudices and preferences.

Whether or not the reader shares these beliefs it is hoped that the text will serve some useful purpose in improving the supports made available to the individuals with developmental disabilities who trouble us with their behavior.

Behavior Recording Charts – Analysis Guide

This is a tool for helping with the analysis of detailed incident records. As the number of incident records increases, so does the need for a more systematic analysis – 'eyeballing' becomes less and less effective as a means of detecting themes and regularities.

This guide will help you to analyze behavior recording charts by categorizing each chart in terms of what it suggests as key events that precede incidents and what may be the function(s) of the behavior that you are trying to understand. Analyzing a number of charts will help you to identify 'strong themes' in the behavior – what the behavior seems to be telling us about the person. This in turn will make it possible to plan and implement programs of support that may help to decrease the behavior of concern.

The guide may be used on a stand-alone basis or in conjunction with the Behavioral Explorer system.

Limitations of the present guide

This guide is just about how to analyze behavior recording charts for meaning. It does not consider broader issues of how we define problematic/challenging behaviors; it is not a comprehensive guide to assessment and intervention.

Principles of the guide

The guide is based upon the following principles:

(a) **Behavior has meaning** – whatever it is that a person does tells us something about the person, their views and preferences, their wants and needs. Behavior 'speaks' to us directly about the person. Most behavior is functional – it will sometimes achieve a change that is important for the person. The behavior is repeated because it has the power to cause this change, often more effectively than any other means that the person has. Following from this, behavior is also tied to circumstances – it is more likely to occur in some situations rather than others.

(b) **Recording behavior objectively helps us to understand it** – we can get a better understanding of behavior if we keep records when the behavior occurs. The most helpful records will be those that note the behavior and things that went on before and after an incident – records that contain a lot of opinion or interpretation of what went on will be less helpful than records that keep a focus on observable events and situations.

(c) **Meaning gets clearer when you analyze a number of recordings** – making sense of each individual recording can be difficult. By looking at a number of records it gets easier to identify themes in behavior – recurring factors that help us to understand what the behavior is often about even if not every single incident fits that analysis. Intervention is better planned around strong themes initially and then reassessing the situation once new supports have been implemented and we can see how far that has taken us.

Steps in analysis

The process of analysis goes through a series of steps:

1. Make sure that there is a system for recording incidents of behavior(s) that give rise to concern.

2. Focus on one specific behavior for analysis – if a person does a number of things that give rise to concern do not try to

analyze them all together and do not cluster them into a single category (such as disturbed, tantrums, aggression, self-injury).

3. Review all the recordings of incidents of this specific behavior and categorize each recording using the systems described below.

4   Calculate the percentages of recordings that fit the specific categories.

5. Start work around those categories that achieve the highest percentage scores (the Behavioral Explorer sets more specific criteria).

6. Update the analysis as you go along – as further incidents are recorded, categorize them, add them to the records already analyzed and adjust the percentages. This will help to identify new themes and will also help to evaluate the programs of support that are being implemented (if they are working, the prominence/percentage score of a theme should decrease).

Category system

Having decided upon a specific behavior to analyze, look at each incident recording and categorize it in a number of ways. We need first to identify the things that commonly precede incidents – *the short-term setting conditions/ecological conditions* and the *triggers/antecedents.*

Short-Term Setting Conditions/Ecological Conditions

Use Analysis Table 1 (see Table A2.1). Use a separate row for each different setting condition identified. For each chart enter a mark in the chart allocation column for the setting conditions identified. When all charts have been examined, work out the percentages of charts that identify particular setting conditions – this will help to indicate the most common such conditions. Feel free to add rows to the table.

Triggers/Antecedents

Use Analysis Table 2 (see Table A2.2). Use a separate row for each different trigger identified. For each chart enter a mark in the chart allocation column for the triggers identified. When all charts have been examined, work out the percentages of charts that identify particular triggers – this will help to indicate the most common such factors. Feel free to add rows to the table.

Results/Consequences

Use Analysis Table 3 (see Table A2.3). Identifying the reinforcers that maintain behavior is a little more complicated. It requires analysis of the whole context of an incident. However, most behaviors are maintained by one of a small number of reinforcing events. Below we try to define these most common reinforcers and give a guide as to the likely contents of a recording that would illustrate the operation of such reinforcement. This will in turn enable you to allocate a chart to one or more of a small number of categories. The categories that we use here are:

- Seeking social support
- Seeking stimulation/mental engagement or focus
- Seeking pressure offset
- On the goody trail
- Other
- Unknown.

SEEKING SOCIAL SUPPORT

Behaviors that are about social support are likely to occur in one or more of the following circumstances:

- *Although there are engaging tasks available the person has not received any social input for some time (has been working independently).*
- *The behavior occurs after the person has been receiving a high level of social support but the level of input has just been decreased – for example, after a period of individual or small group work, after a*

transition from high to lower staff ratio situations, at staff handover times.

- *The behavior occurs in the presence of individuals with whom the person has a strong/significant relationship, at a time when that person's attention is focused elsewhere.*

- *The behavior occurs at transition times when the person has to shift from one activity to another and is not being supported directly at this point of transition.*

SEEKING STIMULATION/MENTAL ENGAGEMENT OR FOCUS

Behaviors that are about seeking stimulation/mental engagement are likely to occur in one or more of the following circumstances:

- *The person has not been actively engaged for some time.*

- *Unstructured times/situations.*

- *Waiting times.*

- *The person has not been offered a prompt to help him to keep focused on the task in hand or offered an alternative task when the task in hand is one that he is known to have difficulty sticking with for any length of time.*

SEEKING PRESSURE OFFSET

Behaviors that are about seeking pressure offset are likely to occur in one or more of the following circumstances:

- *When requests/demands are made on the person.*

- *When others are close or intruding upon the individual's personal space.*

- *When there are arguments/conflicts going on around the person.*

- *When the individual is in a high state of arousal even if the cause is not known.*

- *When the person has been for some time in a situation known to cause discomfort (including being in pain).*

ON THE GOODY TRAIL

Behaviors may help the person access favored materials of one sort or another (food, drinks, cigarettes, favorite activities) in one or more of the following circumstances:

- *The behavior is sometimes followed by something known to be favored by the person…especially if the person rarely initiates access to the 'goody' by any other means.*

- *The behavior occurs after the person has been without favored goodies for some time.*

- *When the person is denied something that she wants.*

- *When the person is waiting for something that is very important to her.*

- *The behavior occurs at the point that a goody that the person has been accessing is coming to an end (for example, end of a meal, end of a favorite video).*

OTHER

Use this category for an incident record that can be understood – it seems clear what contributed to the behavior but it does not fit any of the above categories. Keep summary notes on your interpretation of the incident…this may form the basis for an additional category to add to this list.

UNKNOWN

Use this category when it is not clear at all what contributed to the incident.

Final notes

This approach to analysis can only work when there are a reasonable number of incident records to analyze – 10 recorded incidents would be an absolute minimum, 20 or more would be preferable.

Additional categories can be added in the Results/Consequences Analysis (see notes on 'Other' above) – try to define a category in a way similar to those illustrated above. Write down the definition and apply it to subsequent charts otherwise the definition will 'drift' over time and be less helpful in devising appropriate supports. It may be that with increasing experience you want to change the definition. If you do so it will be necessary to go back and reanalyze all the charts categorized before the definition change, so that they are interpreted in line with the new (and wiser!) definition.

It is always worthwhile trying to get someone not directly involved in day-to-day support to help out with observations of behavior. This can be difficult to effect on a routine basis. However, additional support should definitely be sought under the following circumstances:

- *No particularly strong theme emerges from the incident analysis.*

- *A strong theme emerged, what seemed like appropriate action plans were implemented but no change in behavior occurred.*

- *A large number (30 percent or more) of incident charts are categorized 'UNKNOWN'.*

Table A2.1 Analysis Table 1 Short-term setting/ecological conditions			
SPECIFIC CONDITIONS	CHART ALLOCATION	TOTAL	PERCENTAGE

If using Behavioral Explorer all conditions with a score above 25 percent should be transferred to the appropriate section of the Formulation Guide.

Table A2.2 Analysis Table 2 Triggers/antecedents			
SPECIFIC TRIGGERS	CHART ALLOCATION	TOTAL	PERCENTAGE

If using Behavioral Explorer all conditions with a score above 25 percent should be transferred to the appropriate section of the Formulation Guide.

Table A2.3 Analysis table 3 Reinforcement (results/consequences)			
FUNCTION	**CHART ALLOCATION**	**TOTAL**	**PERCENTAGE**
Seeking social support			
Seeking stimulation/mental engagement or focus			
Seeking pressure offset			
On the goody trail			
Other			
Unknown			

If using Behavioral Explorer all conditions with a score above 10 percent should be transferred to the appropriate section of the Formulation Guide.

Clements Rapid Assessment Protocol

This is an abbreviated version of the Behavioral Explorer. It moves users through gathering information, analyzing it and developing support plans. It can be used as an interview schedule or as a framework for a team organizing and assembling its information, which may be gathered from different sources (for example, rating the functional aspects of behavior might be done after collecting detailed incident records).

A sense of the person

You are on your deathbed...you have two minutes left to live...the person standing next to you is going to support (name) but knows nothing about him/her...what are the main things that you will try to get over in the short time left to you?!

```



```

A sense of the life

What kind of life would work best for this person (doing what, where, with whom and all that good stuff) – what life would be most likely to maximize personal satisfaction and well-being? List out the ways in which the person's current life differs from what you believe to be the ideal.

Personal Resources

Supporters — *list here the people who think well of / like / are prepared to work for / stand up for the individual.*

Communicative competence — *identify here the messages that the person most often tries to get across and how those messages are conveyed (words, looks, gestures, sounds, behaviors).*

Messages:	Conveyed by:

Self-occupational competence – *list here the activities that the individual will engage in for at least ten minutes without encouragement or direction from anyone else.*

```


```

Self-management competence – *list here the things that the person does when becoming increasingly aroused/upset/excited which seem to be about reducing the arousal level or trying to stop behaviors that appear at high arousal levels.*

```


```

Positive well-being – *list here the strong points about the person's health, things that obviously lead to the person feeling happy or relaxed, things that make the person smile or laugh.*

```


```

Analysis Of The Behavior

Identify very specifically the behavior that you want to understand better:

```


```

Rate to what extent this behavior demonstrates the following characteristics (positive functional, negative functional, disinhibitory), using the following 5-point scale:

1. Does not apply at all

2. Might apply

3. Applies to some extent

4. Applies in many instances

5. Applies in almost every instance.

Positive functional characteristics

A behavior has positive functional characteristics when, as a result of the behavior, the individual at least some of the time gets access to a positively preferred situation which he/she might not have got access to if the behavior had not occurred. A behavior would have these characteristics if one or more of the following apply:

- The person likes social support and gets more support after the behavior or gets more support from a preferred person.

- Incidents of behavior are followed by access to preferred food/drink items which would not otherwise have been scheduled.

- The behavior generates types of sensory stimulation that the individual is known to prefer.

- Incidents of behavior are followed by access to preferred activities which would not otherwise have been scheduled.

- Incidents of behavior are preceded by a time period when the individual was without social support and this individual is known to prefer high levels of social support.

- Incidents of behavior are preceded by a time period when the individual was without engaging activities and this individual is known to prefer being actively engaged most of the time.

         1   2   3   4   5

If you rated 3 or higher, list out the specific things that the behavior achieves for the person:

```
┌──────────────────────────────────────────────────┐
│                                                  │
│                                                  │
│                                                  │
│                                                  │
│                                                  │
└──────────────────────────────────────────────────┘
```

Negative functional characteristics

A behavior has negative functional characteristics when, as a result of the behavior, the individual at least some of the time gets out of non-preferred situations and he/she might not have got out of these if the behavior had not occurred. A behavior would have these characteristics if one or more of the following apply:

- The behavior is triggered by demands or denials.

- The behavior occurs in environments that contain elements known to be aversive to the individual (for example, busy, crowded, noisy).

- The behavior occurs when people try to interrupt the individual when he/she is busy doing something else.

- The behavior results in rearrangement of the environment so that non-preferred elements are eliminated (items are removed, eaten, flushed down the toilet, destroyed or otherwise rearranged).

1   2   3   4   5

If you rated 3 or higher, list out the specific things that the behavior gets rid of for the person:

```
┌──────────────────────────────────────────────────┐
│                                                  │
│                                                  │
│                                                  │
│                                                  │
└──────────────────────────────────────────────────┘
```

Disinhibitory characteristics

Some behaviors seem to achieve no meaningful outcome for the individual but rather seem more like a 'loss of control'. A behavior would have these characteristics if one or more of the following apply:

- When we review what we know about this behavior we realize that the conditions that trigger it occur much more often than the behavior itself – most of the time the triggers are coped with and the behavior does not occur; it is successfully inhibited.

- The behavior occurs only when the individual is in a highly aroused state (very angry, very distressed, very high).

- The individual sometimes shows genuine remorse (not a superficial 'sorry') after incidents.

- Close observation reveals that the individual sometimes makes active attempts at self-control (taking self away, sitting on hands or in some other way self-restraining, positioning self behind a desk, asking to leave a situation).

| 1 | 2 | 3 | 4 | 5 |

If you rated 3 or higher, list out the specific things that get the person into a highly aroused state:

| |
| |

Thematic analysis

Here we will rate for the presence of certain key contextual variables that might influence the behavior – the behavior might be part of a more general issue (it might not).

Once again we will use a 5-point rating scale for each factor:

1.   Not present at all

2.   Present to a small extent

3.   Present to some extent

4.   A significant issue

5.   A very significant issue.

Relationship context

We are looking here at whether there is a significant issue about the person's participation in two-way social exchanges, which might be impacting the behavior that concerns us – about the individual's coping with the reciprocal, give and take elements of social relating. This issue may have always been present or the person may have changed over time in this respect. Problems in the relationship context involve one or more of the following situations:

- In some or all environments the person is taking complete control, setting rules for everyone else, being completely intolerant of challenges or demands.

- Frequently in the course of a day the person will do things to control what other people do (make them do/not do certain things) and the focus is more on the exercise of this control rather than the specific things that people are made to do.

- The person has lost all tolerance for requests to cooperate (being asked to do tasks, being asked to stop doing things, being denied things). As long as such requests are absent the person may remain relatively quiet but any social intrusion leads to rapid and intense escalation.

- The person has withdrawn completely and spends nearly all his time in an area or areas that are away from other people.

- The person is completely absorbed for most of the time in self-generated, repetitive activities and is very hard to distract or redirect from these.

- The person makes no initiations to others – no issues are brought to the notice of others by any means whatsoever.

     1   2   3   4   5

If you rated 3 or higher, list out the specific relationship issues:

Communication context

We are looking here at whether there is a significant issue about our competence at communicating with each other, which might be impacting the behavior that concerns us – about whether information passes successfully between us. This issue may have always been present or the person may have changed over time in this respect. Problems in the communication context involve one or more of the following situations:

- The person gets ideas about what is going to happen which are different from what is actually going to happen and this leads to conflict.

- When we review what we know of the person and her life it seems quite possible that she has no real understanding of what happens when.

- Transitions are very difficult.

- The person is completely thrown by any change in routine and seems to rely on learning activity sequences by heart to make sense of the world.

- The person does have important issues and does try to get them across. However, the means used to communicate are not typical (not words, signs, pictures) and communication only succeeds if you are watching the person closely and know her well.

1   2   3   4   5

If you rated 3 or higher, list out the specific areas/issues in which communication breaks down:

```



```

Well-being context

We are looking here at whether there is a significant issue about personal well-being, which might be impacting the behavior that concerns us. The issue might involve short-term fluctuations in well-being (for example, moods within a day, temporary health issues such as sinus problems or constipation). There may also be longer-term fluctuations/cycles lasting weeks or months (mood cycles, extended health problems). Problems in the well-being context involve one or more of the following situations:

- The person experiences elevated arousal levels and the behavior is more likely in this state.

- Problems occur more often at the common human biorhythmic down times (early morning, mid afternoon).

- The person rarely smiles or laughs happily (as opposed to manically).

- You can tell that the person is in a negative mood state and when you observe this state you have evidence that behavior is more likely.

- The person has lost tolerance for things (for example, noises) that she used to tolerate.

- The person seems very driven to complete certain action sequences and gets very upset if he is interrupted.

- The person has recurring health problems and, when these are present, behavior is impacted.
- The person is edgy/anxious a lot of the time.
- The person is not sleeping for two or three nights in succession.
- The person has daily outbursts of intense emotion, not always for reasons that others can understand.
- The person seems unable to do, say or understand things that he used to be able to do, say, understand.
- The person is choosing to spend more time alone/in isolation.
- The person is communicating much less often than he used to.

If you rated 3 or higher, list out the specific well-being issues:

```



```

Bringing it together

The behavior of concern is:

```



```

On the basis of our assessment we believe that the following specific factors are contributing to this behavior:

1.

2.

3.

4.

5.

6.

7.

8.

9.

And therefore it would be logical for us to take the following actions:

Making the promise

We hereby agree to offer the following supports to (name) that we believe will improve personal satisfaction and well-being and reduce behavior:

And we will monitor this plan for its effectiveness by:

Signed on this the   day of   in the year

by

Resources

Carr, E.G., Horner, R.H., Turnbull, A.P. and colleagues (1999) *Positive Behavior Support for People with Developmental Disabilities. A Research Synthesis.* Washington: AAMR.

Clements, J. (1997) 'Challenging Needs and Problematic Behavior.' In J. O'Hara and A. Sperlinger (eds) *Adults with Learning Disabilities. A Practical Approach for Health Professionals.* Chichester: John Wiley & Sons.

Clements, J. and Zarkowska, E. (2000) *Behavioural Concerns and Autistic Spectrum Disorders: Explanations and Strategies for Change.* London: Jessica Kingsley.

Dinerstein, R.D., Herr, S.S. and O'Sullivan, J.L. (eds) (1999) *A Guide about Consent.* Washington: AAMR.

Emerson, E. (2002) *Challenging Behaviour: Analysis and Intervention in People with Learning Disabilities.* Cambridge: Cambridge University Press.

Lucyshyn, J.M., Dunlap. G. and Albin, R. W. (2002) *Families and Positive Behavior Support: Addressing Problem Behavior in Family Context.* Baltimore: Brookes.

Martin, N., Gaffan, E.A. and Williams, T. (1999) 'Experimental Functional Analyses for Challenging Behavior: A Study of Validity and Reliability.' *Research in Developmental Disabilities 20, 2, 125–146.*

Martin, N., Oliver, C. and Hall, S. (2000) *ObsWin – Observational Data Collection & Analysis* (software). London: Antam Ltd.

O'Neill, R.E., Horner, R.H., Albin, R.W., Sprague, J.R., Storey, K. and Newton, J.S. (1997) *Functional Assessment and Program Development for Problem Behavior. A Practical Handbook.* Pacific Grove: Brooks/Cole.

Schalock, R.L. (ed) (1996) *Quality of Life. Volume 1. Conceptualization and Measurement.* Washington: AAMR.

Schalock, R.L. (ed) (1997) *Quality of Life. Volume 2. Applications to Persons with Disabilities.* Washington: AAMR.

Thompson, T., Felce, D. and Symons, F.J. (eds) (2000) *Behavioral Observation: Technology and Applications in Developmental Disabilities.* Baltimore: Brookes.

Person centered planning – a very useful website

http://www.allenshea.com

Index

Abuse 15, 30, 97, 112, 183
Access 140, 201
Accountability 185
Action Cycle 23–24, 118–9
Activities *see* Influences on behavior
  – short term
Analog Assessment 76–8, 182
Antecedents (*see also* Influences on
  behavior – immediate, short
  term) 46, 48–9, 58, 104, 105,
  115, 134–5, 208, 212
Arousal 47, 49, 54, 104, 107, 109,
  111, 112, 115, 149, 150, 159,
  216, 222
Attitudes 24

Behavior plans 180, 183–199
Behavior stability 21–2, 201
Behavioral Explorer Chapter 6 and
  73, 96, 143, 205, 207, 212,
  213, 214
Biorhythms 50, 58, 149, 222

Celebration 27, 118
Communication skills 34, 35, 53,
  57, 93–4, 112, 116, 117, 130,
  147, 148, 150, 158, 164, 169,
  170, 172–3, 215, 221–2
Conflict (*see also* Influences on
  behavior – longer term) 111
Consent 15, 19–20, 142
Consequences *see* Reinforcement
Consistency 184

Control issues (*see also* Power issues)
  18, 53, 91, 147, 163–4

Dangerousness 25
Defining Behavior 24, 42–3, 66–7,
  124–6, 144, 186, 189, 194,
  216
Devaluation 17, 18, 36
Discriminative Stimuli 48, 104, 106
Disinhibition *see* Inhibition

Ecological Conditions *see* Influences
  on behavior – short term
Emotion (*see also* Mood) 24, 39, 50,
  51, 58, 85–6, 96, 111–2, 130,
  131, 147, 148, 160, 169, 170,
  182
Emotional Management 54, 57,
  94–5, 112, 116, 130, 216
Empathy, Chapter 2
Environmental conditions *see*
  Influences on behavior
Establishing Operations (*see also*
  Influences on behavior – short
  term) 48–9, 104, 107, 109,
  111
Ethical Issues (*see also* Consent)
  165–6, 178, 201–202
Everyday Life 201

Formulation *see* Working theory

Hassles *see* Life events
Hypothesizing *see* Working theory

Influences on behavior
  immediate 46–9, 58, 68–82,
    104–8, 130, 133, 134–5,
    180, 190, 195–6, 208,
    212–3, 217–9

226

Note: This book deals entirely with gathering and analysis of information about behavior. It did not therefore prove useful to index the topics 'Assessment' and 'Analysis' of behavior